Introduction to Christian Camping

Introduction to Christian Camping

Edited by

Werner C. Graendorf

and

Lloyd D. Mattson

Camping Guideposts
Duluth, Minnesota

Library of Congress Cataloging in Publication Data
Main entry under title:
Introduction to Christian Camping
  Includes bibliographies.
  1. Church camps. 2. Camps—Administration.
1. Graendorf, Werner C. II. Mattson, Lloyd D.
BV1650.153   254'.6   78-10284
ISBN 0-942684-07-9

Second Printing, 1980
Second Edition, 1984

Photos supplied by Camp Haluwasa, Hammonton, NJ
Published by Camping Guideposts, 5118 Glendale St., Duluth, MN
55804
Printed in the United States of America

Contents

CHAPTER | PAGE

Foreword 7

About This Book 9

How to Use This Book 11

Unit I—CHRISTIAN CAMPING FOUNDATIONS

1. Camping Purpose—*Werner C. Graendorf* 15
2. Camping History—*Clifford V. Anderson* 33
3. Forms of Camping—*Lloyd D. Mattson* 49

Unit II—CHRISTIAN CAMPING PROGRAM

4. Program Principles—*James R. Crosby* 65
5. Program Activities—*James R. Crosby* 79
6. Arts and Crafts—*James Rands* 95
7. Specialized Programs—*P. Richard Bunger* 109
8. Training Programs: A Case Study—*Wesley E. Harty* 121

Unit III—CHRISTIAN CAMP STAFFING

9. Staff Personnel—*Wesley R. Willis* 133
10. Building the Camp Staff—*Harold J. Westing* 147
11. Camp Counseling: Understanding Campers—*Joy Mackay* 157
12. Camp Counseling: Working with Campers—
    J. Omar Brubaker 171

Unit IV—CHRISTIAN CAMP MANAGEMENT

13. Sponsorship and Organization—*Lloyd D. Mattson* 189
14. Camp Facilities—*C. June Stump* 199
15. Professional Camp Leadership—*Bill V. Bynum* 211
    Appendix 223

Foreword

"A camp setting is the greatest environment for learning today."

—Dr. Ted Ward*

I have wished for a long time that Christian colleges and camp directors could have a textbook on Christ-centered camping that would give an up-to-date treatment of camping as a vital arm of the church and church-related youth organizations. I feel this new camping textbook will give that kind of responsible overview.

The textbook is a symposium bringing together the thoughts and experiences of thirteen writers. Two knowledgeable camping leaders, Werner Graendorf and Lloyd Mattson, have done a masterful work in selecting topics and writers to give a thorough treatment of the major facets of Christian camping.

Growing government demands and legislation in the area of youth camping have made evident that Christian camps need to set their sights toward quality camping and become examples of excellence in this field. This book will help support the initiatives Christian camping has taken toward safer and more excellent camping.

As you study these chapters my sincere prayer is that you seize the opportunities before you in the unique ministry of Christian camping.

EDWARD OULAND
Executive Director
Christian Camping International

*Michigan State University professor and international educational consultant for the Carnegie Foundation, in a speech before the international convention of Christian Camping International, Green Lake, Wisconsin.

Preface to the Second Edition

The idea for this book took shape in 1975 as I surveyed the literature of Christian camping. I could find no current discussion of the backgrounds, philosophy, and program concepts that are shaping the growing Christian camping movement. I presented the idea to the editors of Moody Press, and they assigned Dr. Werner Graendorf to assist with the project.

Many months were given to building the outline, recruiting competent writers, rewriting and editing, and finally presenting the manuscript to the publisher. The first edition appeared in 1979 and it met with immediate acceptance. A second printing in 1980 served the growing number of Christian schools becoming involved in camping education.

In 1983 the copyright was assigned to Camping Guideposts, a publishing house established to provide resources for Christian camps and conferences. This second edition of AN INTRODUCTION TO CHRISTIAN CAMPING has been released as an interim edition to supply the demand while a more thorough revision and updating is underway. Changes are taking place in our world which affect the camping ministry significantly.

Camping remains the most effective environment for education, spiritual discovery, and personal growth available to the church today. We're pleased to add AN INTRODUCTION TO CHRISTIAN CAMPING to the growing list of resources designed to help leaders as they serve the cause of Christ through camping.

Lloyd Mattson
Camping Guideposts
Duluth, MN
1984

About This Book

Before *Introduction to Christian Camping* was initiated, one of the editors asked a Midwest camp leader what he thought would be of greatest help in strengthening the Christian camping movement.

The leader gave a very practical reply: the publication of a basic textbook that would provide a clear understanding of the meaning and essentials of Christian camping today.

This reply expressed well the purpose of this book: to serve as an introductory guide to Christian camping, its meaning, and essentials.

The areas included in the book reflect in large measure the thinking of the Christian camping community. Suggestions for and reactions to the proposed book were garnered from Christian camps, conferences, and fellowships. A substantial school survey was conducted by Larry McCullough of Columbia Bible College, and well over one hundred institutions across the United States and Canada responded. Christian Camping International has given helpful support to the publication.

Many more topics, of course, might have been included. We have already had suggestions for added chapters on golfing camps and camp director retirement camps! (Seriously, the editors will welcome recommendations for future inclusion.)

We have enjoyed our work with the eleven men and women who shared in the writing. While there has been a basic format and common philosophy, the varied backgrounds and individuality of the writers has greatly enriched the scope of the material.

We believe this book provides a sound text for introductory camping courses and a basic resource for all who are involved with or are interested in the Christian camping movement.

Because we believe that camping is one of God's choice tools for His work today, we happily commit these pages to the extension of that work.

WERNER C. GRAENDORF
LLOYD D. MATTSON

How to Use This Book

This book is designed as a text for courses in Christian camping. Several features have been built into the text with course instruction in mind:

First, the material is divided into *four units*, each related to a major area of camping. The several chapters in each unit develop the unit topic.

The units follow a logical development, beginning with a basic *introduction to the subject* of Christian camping in Unit 1. The second unit focuses on the *program* of Christian camping, the third emphasizes the *camper*, and Unit 4 relates to the *operation* of the camp.

Again, each chapter begins with a simple *outline* of what the chapter covers. Each chapter also affords *study helps* composed of suggested questions and/or projects. Recommended resources are included, some as part of the chapter footnoting.

The outlining and study helps are planned also to aid the person doing personal study or using the book as a camping resource.

The following are suggestions for using *Introduction to Christian Camping* in the classroom:

1. The book can be used as a *course framework*, and the chapters followed as the outline of the course.
2. It may be treated as a *course resource*, and the chapters used with a course outline as material for the individual areas being considered.
3. When the book is used as a *course reference*, chapters may be referred to for special emphases or recommended reading.
4. The material is adaptable to courses of varied length. There is a

11

sufficient base here for *three-hour* courses; however, consideration has also been given *two-hour* courses, where it may be
necessary to leave out some chapters or to use them as reference
reading. Each instructor has fifteen chapters to evaluate for this
purpose.

For the simplest introduction to Christian camping, chapters
1, 3, 4, and 9 provide a broad base. Other chapters then fill in
essential areas to give a full understanding of the subject.

Unit 1

Christian Camping Foundations

The foundation for any kind of camping is its *purpose*. Purpose establishes whether a camp is geared to purely recreational fun or to more serious educational accomplishments. Purpose determines the direction a camp will take as to personnel, programming, and facilities. Christian camping has the added dimension of *biblical* purpose, which implies that spiritual, eternal values will grow out of the camping experience.

Camping today has developed out of the camping experiences of the past, and camping *history* provides the basis for understanding the roots and growth of the camping movement. Nowhere can one find a more fascinating history or richer heritage for ministry than in the pioneer trails of the Christian camping movement.

Finally, camping has expressed itself through a wide range of *forms*, from highly developed resident settings to the wilderness trail. Behind the forms lie basic organizational patterns that reflect both the history and philosophy of Christian camping.

This unit is designed to introduce you to what Christian camping is, and how it came to be this way. These chapters written by Werner C. Graendorf, Clifford V. Anderson, and Lloyd D. Mattson provide a key for foundational thinking on the Christian camping movement around the world.

1

Camping Purpose

Werner C. Graendorf

WERNER C. GRAENDORF (Ph.D., New York University) is chairman of the Department of Christian Education and professor of Christian education, Moody Bible Institute, Chicago, Illinois. Dr. Graendorf has been camp director in Christian Service Brigade in various parts of the country; state director of camping, Conservative Baptist Association of Southern California; and active with Forest Home (Calif.) camping program.

- *The Identification of Christian Camping*
- *The Relationship of Christian Camping to Church Ministry*
- *The Distinctive Purpose of Christian Camping*

Camping—the word with universal appeal![1] For most of us it readily lends itself to happy visions of open sky, cheerful campfires, and, generally, living at its simplest best—even though the actual experience may not always be that ideal.

However viewed, camping and camps today represent a substantial feature and influence in our way of life.[2] While usually considered in a recreational context, camping has significant impact in other areas such as educational and social work, as well as being a major economic force. And the indications are strong that in an increasingly technology-oriented society, the camping appeal and influence will continue to grow. This includes the church area.[3]

It seems imperative, therefore, for those concerned with contemporary Christianity to give fresh study to the place of camping in the ministry of today's church. In a Christian perspective, where does camping fit, and what should it do?

Such considerations, it should immediately be noted, are no longer a simple matter of assessing the outdoor experience of children. Camping rightfully understood has significant implications for a wide spectrum of contemporary church life and renewal, in addition to the traditional children-youth emphasis.

The potential of camp ministry in such areas as family life, senior citizens, discipleship, body life, and the whole range of mentally

---

1. "To young people the word *camping* suggests adventure and excitement—a different life which can be chosen for leisure time, something to do away from home or school and old familiar rounds. Our young country still lives near in time to frontier life when every trip west was a camping out." (American Camping Association (ACA), *Camping IS Education* [Ind.: ACA, 1960], p. 9.)

2. Robert E. McBride, for example, has predicted: "The time is not too far off when a camping experience will be considered a normal part of the educational and recreational experience of every American child." (Robert E. McBride, *Camping at the Mid-Century* [n.p.: ACA, 1953], p. 24.)

3. "During the past few years, practically all the major church denominations have developed some type of camping program. Camping . . . is probably the newest and fastest growing trend or phase of Christian education." (William H. Freeberg and Loren E. Taylor, *Philosophy of Outdoor Education* [Minneapolis: Burgess, 1961], p. 194.)

and physically handicapped offers a deeply challenging opportunity
for study and development. The existing pioneering programs in
specialized and innovative Christian camping graphically illustrate
the possibilities.[4]
The *broad* question of church involvement in camping has already, of course, a basic logistic answer. Each year thousands of
churches and church workers *are* involved in some aspect of camping. Camp facilities represent a major investment of churches and
church-related organizations.[5] Each year, for better or for worse,
increasing hundreds of children, young people, and adults are having a Christian camping experience.[6] But the concern in this chapter represents a deeper consideration than simply registration figures, acreage, or similar areas.

True, organized camping does involve facilities, programs, and
counselors, and these are considered in later chapters. However,
before money is spent, camp programs set up, or counselors arranged for, there is an essential first step in effective camping. It is
the understanding of camp purpose. That step is critical.

The nature of the camping experience (as many of us remember
from personal involvement) lends itself to emotional response and
ofttimes euphoric evaluation. In the camp setting it is relatively easy
to settle for dramatic campfires and immediate results. In effect, the
camping experience can become a happy end in itself and accomplishment be left up on the mountain or beside the lake.

Yet, for the person who takes time to understand and plan for
what camping is actually capable of producing, there is a gripping
potential of solid, long-range accomplishment, as campers and camp
leaders everywhere can attest.

We are talking here about the reason for doing *Christian* camping. We know that camping is enjoyable recreational activity—
wholesome and outdoor oriented. That is one of its attractive,
legitimate strengths. Camping is fun.

We also know that camping has great social appeal. What better
place than a camp for enjoying fellowship around the campfire,
camaraderie under the blue sky, or just plain mess hall joviality!

---

4. Such as Camp Hope for handicapped and retarded children in New
   York, begun by Win Ruelke in the early 1950s.
5. Christian Camping International (CCI) estimates that the United
   States-Canada combined investment exceeds 1.5 billion dollars.
6. This is indicated, for example, by the CCI-Scripture Press joint research study of camping trends involving over one thousand Christian
   camps in 1970. (*Research Report on Christian Camping Activities and
   Trends* [Wheaton, Ill.: Scripture Press, 1970].)

Camping has many such appeals, ranging from simple adventure to the possible leadership expectation of concentrated teaching time.

Yet the Christian goes further. While he believes in recreation, fellowship, and the other varied appeals inherent in the camping experience, he also sees in camping a tool, a potent, dynamic tool, for doing God's work. And he earnestly seeks camping's place in the fulfilling of the Great Commission for our day.

In effect, the person sincerely interested in *Christian* camping and the productive use of its funds, programs, and people will want a biblical approach to camping; call it a philosophy if you will. Such a person desires a clear understanding of Bible-based purpose for the camp and its operational policies.

Developing basic direction in the areas of definition, church relationship, and purpose not only will assist us to determine what to expect through the camping experience, but also, just as crucially, will guide us in taking action toward achieving these expectations. Facilities, staffing, programming—every aspect of camping— eventually reflect a camping philosophy. Thus, while it is not the purpose of this chapter to provide a finely detailed camping strategy, guidelines for productive biblical thinking about Christian camping are suggested.

For many this will mean opportunity to evaluate and reinforce already established direction. For the student and person new to the camping field, the chapter will offer basic building material.

The Identification of Christian Camping

According to its most basic definition, camping is simply outdoor living. As such, camping can run the gamut from the boy with his blanket and tin can stove in the backyard to the family in its luxury trailer at Yellowstone National Park.

However, when we add stated objectives and establish program direction under qualified leadership, we move into the area of *organized camping*. Normally, we are now also concerned with group living. Thus, the American Camping Association identifies camping as "an experience in group living in a natural environment. It is a sustained experience under the supervision of trained leadership."[7]

The *forms* that organized camping takes cover a wide spectrum of age levels, interest areas, organization, and programming emphases (discussed in chaps. 3 and 4). Form, for example, may range from a highly structured resident camp to the stress orientation of an ele-

---

7. ACA, *Camping IS Education*, p. 8.

mental wilderness experience.

But beyond simply noting definitions and forms as such, we are here concerned with a very particular dimension of the camping enterprise, namely *Christian* camping.

Some might prefer the term *church* camping, and indeed this has validity. In a large sense we are concerned with camping as it relates to the body of Christ represented by the local church. Actually there can be no Christian camping without the church in this sense, that is, without the involvement of local believers.

However, for our purpose we are using the term *Christian* as the broadest designation for the type of camping being discussed. We thus include camping that, while it may not be sponsored by an organized church body as such, is distinctly Christian in its purpose and leadership because it builds its philosophy on biblical foundations.

Here, then, the definition developed by an evangelical camping committee some years ago is still usable: "Christian camping may be defined as an experience in Christian living in the out-of-doors under guidance."[8]

The fuller understanding of Christian camping, of course, must go beyond descriptive definition. It must also be concerned with functional context, or the relationship in which the camping experience takes place. A prime consideration here is the local church, and this moves us directly into our second philosophy area.

THE RELATIONSHIP OF CHRISTIAN CAMPING TO CHURCH MINISTRY

Perhaps as essential as any other single factor in the fullest utilization of Christian camping is the establishing and understanding of its status as basic Christian education and as a key ministry in the church's educational program.[9] This means camp is more than simply a wholesome supplementary activity on a church's summer (or winter) calendar. It means understanding camping as the *church* ministering to its people and community.

Betty van der Smissen states: "The camp program is an aspect of

---

8. Developed for the National Sunday School Association (NSSA) Camp Commission, 1960, and identified in Floyd Todd and Pauline Todd, *Camping for Christian Youth* (New York: Harper & Row, 1963), p. 33.
9. Most of the educational implications of this chapter are drawn from the author's "Criteria for Establishing an Educational Philosophy for a Church-related Camp" (M.S. thesis, University of Southern California, 1964).

the church's Christian education program."[10] Similarly, John and Ruth Ensign introduce *Camping Together as Christians* by referring to camping as "an integral part of the program of Christian education."[11]

By its nature, as well as by its historical development (see chap. 2), camping carries a heavy recreational connotation. Often this provides not only its wholesome appeal but also its overriding, major concern. (A case in point is the camp that justifiably boasts of its highly trained and qualified waterfront staff, yet has on its *counseling* staff a number of members randomly recruited shortly before camp opening.) Christian camping is far more than good recreation. With all of its healthy capacity for fun, camping is still to be viewed as a tool rather than merely a toy.

This recognition of the Christian camp as Christian education provides first of all a *proper relationship between means and ends.* The programs of the Christian camp are not ends in themselves; they provide unique opportunities for fulfilling goals of edification and evangelism. Accordingly, the Camp Commission of the National Sunday School Association began its recommendations for a Christian camping philosophy by noting that the goals of Christian camping "must be in line with the basic goals of Christian education, as set forth in the Word of God . . . [and] must relate the camp ministry to that of the home and local church."[12] Here is little place for diverging flow of time and effort on the part of camp and church. Rather, what is called for is a potent channeling of multiple effort toward common goals.

A second implication of camping as Christian education is *provision for total ministry.* Where the church recognizes camping as the church in action, and camping is established as a vital part of that action, we move toward productive, continuing effort. "Camp . . . is just part of a total year's program for the campers."[13] "The local church should tie the camp experience into its total program."[14] In this approach, camp follow-through is not something added or not added to the program. (It is not difficult to remember, for example, the teenagers at senior high church camp who responded to the

10. Betty van der Smissen, *The Church Camp Program* (Newton, Kans.: Faith and Life, 1961), p. 4.
11. John Ensign and Ruth Ensign, *Camping Together as Christians* (Richmond: John Knox, 1958), Foreword.
12. Camp Commission, NSSA *Guiding Principles for Christian Camping* (Chicago: NSSA, 1962), p. 8.
13. Ibid., p. 17.
14. van der Smissen, p. 4.

messages of a dedicated missionary—their commitment to possible missionary service deeply sincere. Nor to also remember that when some of these came back to camp the following summer it became obvious that church concern and guidance for the growth of their missionary interest had not gotten beyond the campsite gate. It had been strictly a camp experience.)

Understood as Christian education, camping becomes a key part of a *total* ministry whose results are planned for, anticipated, and are part of an ongoing effort. Here Sunday school and camp point toward common goals. *Each* part of the church's program strengthens the other parts. The camp's missionary challenge now becomes one phase of the church's overall missionary program for its youth and is treated accordingly.

The growth of such productive camp-church relationships is not accidental. It comes from continuing effort by church leadership that is as much concerned with people as with program. It must also be a two-way street. It is relatively easy for the camping professional, often impatient with church administration and "flatlander" ways, to live within his own world of outdoor individualism and kindred camping spirits. He is tempted to build his own goals and develop his own ministry.

On the other hand, church leadership is not without its difficulties in building proper camping perspective. Camping has had to struggle to establish its identity as a total living experience rather than a closely structured conference-type program. Here, perhaps, is a reflection of what Gene Getz has referred to as "institutionalism"—in this case the unwillingness of church leadership at times to encourage the development of camping's own unique potential.[15]

Now it is true that camping is special, as John and Ruth Ensign point out: "The church-sponsored camp . . . provides opportunities for Christian learning and guidance that cannot be achieved elsewhere in the church's program of Christian education."[16]

Camping *is* unique, yet camping's ultimate effectiveness lies not in its uniqueness but in terms of uniquely fulfilling an established purpose that relates to the church's total ministry. It is essential, then, in a final philosophical area to identify such purpose.

15. Gene A. Getz, *Sharpening the Focus of the Church* (Chicago: Moody, 1974), pp. 202-210.
16. Ensign and Ensign, p. 7.

THE DISTINCTIVE PURPOSE OF CHRISTIAN CAMPING

In seeking to establish camping purpose, it is logical to turn to camping values. In the Christian camp, as in the secular camp, there are values inherent in the camping experience itself. These range from the healthy outdoor setting to the benefit of guided group living. The Christian camp does not ignore these, and it does well to include in its statement of objectives such areas as healthful living, appreciation of nature, community spirit, self-reliance, and similar objectives based on camp values.

Notice that we have used the term *objectives* here. These are not the same as *purpose*. Objectives we consider to be statements of those things a camp desires to accomplish as part of its overall purpose. "To enable the camper to identify the plant and wildlife of the camp area" is an example of an objective based on the camp value of being in an outdoor setting. It is not, however, the major purpose for the camp's existence.

Each camp will have its own statement of objectives. These will relate to its particular areas of program emphasis (e.g., trail camping), age group setting (e.g., high schoolers), and sponsoring body teaching (e.g., church missionary emphasis). A trail camping program could well include the objective to have the campers develop basic backpacking skills.[17]

But beyond any statement of objectives is the overall *purpose*, or guiding philosophy, of the camp. Here we look at the compass point that provides the vital direction for camp program, staffing, and major operational policies. A music camp's overall purpose could be in terms of developing outstanding musicians, while an objective might be for each camper to read two biographies of musicians.

The purpose for Christian camping begins with a spiritual orientation. As tribute, perhaps, to the native wholesomeness of camping is the fact that there has been wide recognition of its spiritual potential. For example, a leading secular camping text, by A. Viola Mitchell and Ida B. Crawford, included in its chapter on objectives (2d ed.) the general note that camp has great spiritual values. These authors

---

17. Robert Pickens Davis lists "special contributions of the church camp," which provide helpful guidance for building camp objectives, in Robert Pickens Davis, *Church Camping* (Richmond: John Knox, 1969), p. 14. An excellent basic listing of objectives for evangelical camping is found in NSSA's *Guiding Principles for Christian Camping*, pp. 8-9.

further emphasized group Christian living and the voice of God in nature.[18]

The Christian camp's spiritual orientation, of course, moves beyond this into biblical specifics. Before considering these, however, one other factor besides the spiritual must be noted as we think of Christian camp purpose.

If camping is to be a productive *Christian education* ministry, its purpose must correlate with overall Christian education purpose. We are, therefore, looking for *educational* as well as spiritual orientation. With due allowance for each camp's individual objectives, what can we say is Christian camping's basic spiritual-educational purpose?

An authoritative source gives the answer. Christian camping, as all Christian ministry, has an ultimate authority in the written Word of God (2 Tim. 3:16) as well as an ultimate example in the person of Jesus Christ (1 Pet. 2:21).

---

18. A. Viola Mitchell and Ida B. Crawford, *Camp Counseling*, 2d ed. (Philadelphia: Saunders, 1961), p. 33. There is also a fine discussion of education for spiritual growth in ACA's *Camping IS Education*, pp. 17-21.

As we study the Scriptures, especially the record of the life of Jesus Christ, we do find both spiritual and educational direction.[19] In the educational area, it is evident from Christ's life that a substantial part of His ministry was carried out as an educator. Some ninety references to Him as teacher (or teaching) make this clear. His followers and the community in which He worked regarded Him as a teacher (e.g., John 3:2). His personal testimony was explicit (John 13:13). Jesus Christ was the master educator.

Consequently, we may look to Christ's ministry for guidance in educational purpose, and this is not difficult to find. The testimony of all four gospels is quite clear: Christ's teaching ministry focused on the *making of disciples*.[20] The early call of twelve followers and the training of these represented the Teacher's basic thrust. As Dwight Pentecost in his study of discipleship points out:

> Throughout His ministry Jesus Christ was occupied with making disciples. His ministry was devoted to teaching and training men that these men might be His disciples. From among those who called themselves disciples of the Pharisees and from among others who called themselves disciples of John, and from those who called themselves disciples of Moses, our Lord called men to be disciples of Jesus Christ. His earthly life was invested in these men that they might be His disciples and that they might do the work of a disciple.[21]

This educational purpose of discipleship has been further firmly established for the church by Christ's specific directive in Matthew 28:19-20: "Go therefore and make disciples . . . teaching them."

The development of discipleship—becoming a mature follower of Jesus Christ—includes the basics of the Christian faith. This is indicated as one studies the discipling work of Christ. In Luke 5:1-11, as one example, Christ's discipling includes a teaching foundation in the Word of God, awareness of sin, faith in Christ, and Christian service.

Contrary to some usage, discipleship is by no means merely a romanticized term in Christian literature. Discipleship represents a

---

19. A fuller development of this study can be found in "Teaching for Discipleship," the author's course notes for Contemporary Christian Education.

20. Matt. 5:1-2; Luke 5:1-11; John 1:35-43.

21. J. Dwight Pentecost, *Design for Discipleship* (Grand Rapids: Zondervan, 1971) p. 13. A helpful study on Christ as discipler.

demanding, productive, personal relationship to Christ that is at the very heart of biblical Christianity.[22]

In summary, it is evident from both Christ's example as an educator and His direct command that in Christian education (including the camping area) the making of disciples is a biblical, ultimate purpose.

Let us state this in a camping context: *The overall purpose of Christian camping is to use as fully as possible the camp experience as an opportunity for discipling individuals toward maturity in Christ.*

The statement itself is simple. But when applied as a guiding philosophy, the implications for camping program and operation are deep, dynamic, and challenging. Note some of the practical applications.

The essence of discipling, historically and etymologically, is teaching by example as well as by word. So while we have the record of Christ's *words* to His disciples, as in Matthew 5, at the very heart of His work with these disciples was the directive *"Follow Me"* and the daily living experience that it represented (John 1:43). This was true also of the apostle Paul, who emphasized to the Corinthians, "Be imitators of me, just as I also am of Christ" (1 Cor. 11:1). A major element in discipleship is demonstration.

It is here that the genius of camping as applied Christian education comes dramatically into its own. Christian camping provides the church with what may be its most effective opportunity, outside of the Christian family, for a true discipling ministry. Camping and discipleship are an ideal partnership.

Each of the four major camping distinctives[23] ties directly into discipling:

1. *The twenty-four-hour living experience* of camping provides an environment similar to that of Christ's discipling. It offers ideal daily opportunity for development of Christian living in the normal routines of life. As in the time of Christ, here is place for the questions and interactions that arise naturally in a day's expe-

---

22. As delineated in such material as William MacDonald, *True Discipleship* (Kansas City, Kans.: Walterick, 1962); Geoffrey Bingham, *Cross Without Velvet* (Chicago: Moody, 1960); and A.B. Bruce, *The Training of the Twelve* (New York: Hodder and Stoughton, 1871).

23. Consensus distinctives reflected, for example, in the ACA definition of camping. See also the discussion of camping's unique characteristics in Mitchell, Crawford, and Robberson, pp. 42-48; ACA, *Camp Administration* (Martinsville, Ind.: ACA, 1961), p. 4; and NSSA *Guiding Principles for Christian Living*, pp. 3-6.

riences. Christianity can move from the polite atmosphere of the church building to the give and take of everyday existence. Christian teaching becomes experiential.

2. A second distinctive of organized camping is the factor of *group living*. Here is the opportunity to live and learn with a peer group. The discipling process of the followers of Christ was sharpened by their interrelationships. There was the warmth of Spirit-guided koinonia love as well as the personality-honing abrasiveness of very human living. The Christian camping experience provides rich opportunity for the body life of 1 Corinthians 12 to have expression and development.

3. As vital as any distinctive in Christian camping is the factor of *qualified adult leadership*. Camping offers the opportunity for mature men and women to lead and counsel campers in a wide variety of areas and ways. Significantly, at the center of the discipling process is example ("Follow Me"). What unparalleled opportunity for the prepared Christian counselor to teach the meaning of Christian experience not only by word but also, as in the prototype, Christ, by his life.

4. A final camp distinctive is *outdoor environment*. Again, there is a parallel to the discipling of Christ. While we must not confuse a cultural norm with twentieth-century organized camping, it is clear that Christ's ministry was enhanced by environmental features that are common to camping today. The reflective nature of the discipling process, where illustration and openness have a place, is encouraged by natural setting. Thus lakes, trees, and the world of nature in general were prominent in the ministry of our Lord, as they can be in a contemporary camp.

Christian camping has inherent within it both setting and provision for fully productive discipling. It can offer relatively unpressured, ideal environment, concentrated time periods, mature leadership, and a normative living experience for demonstration and application.

Here is soul-gripping potential for the changing and molding of lives, whether young or old, toward a Christlikeness that is the mark of effective discipling. Here is opportunity for a unified Christian education ministry that, under the guidance and empowering of the Holy Spirit, can implement the growth and renewal that makes a vibrant Christian community. The practical possibilities are almost unlimited.

Where is there greater opportunity, for example, for building and deepening Christian family life than in the well-planned *family camping* experience that provides relaxed environment and time for demonstration and learning?

Again, the whole area of work with the physically and mentally *handicapped* lends itself supremely to camping experiences based on the discipleship distinctives of personalized concern, patience, and demonstrated love. These same distinctives similarly provide rewarding camp ministry for *senior citizens*. For those willing, the challenge of cross-bearing discipleship finds response and training in the demands of *stress camping*.

No matter what the emphasis, the leadership of Christian camping must be clear about its purpose and what the effective outworking of that purpose involves. There are basic discipleship guidelines that provide overall direction for the type of camping presented here.

Primary among these is a *concern for individuals*. Discipleship is by its nature an individual relationship. This means that *the focus of camp experience is on the camper*—knowing him, guiding him, scheduling for him, programming for him, utilizing each facet of the camp experience for his personal maturing.

In a culture characterized by automation and impersonalization, the church also finds itself losing individuals in program schedules and numbers involvement. Here the discipleship approach in camping reminds us of a Christ who spent time with the Peters and Johns and Philips. Camping so understood and organized provides those precious opportunities for knowing and guiding individuals.

The applications here are vast: A Sunday school teacher in camp gets to know his junior highers as Jims and Sandras having personal needs rather than as members of a disinterested class; a father in family camp spends enough informal time with his young son to have the boy express concern for a school drug situation; a shy primary girl needs a patient camp counselor to whom she can unburden her heart, seared with lack of family love.

A camping philosophy focused on a discipling purpose provides—and demands—practical direction in every area of the camping endeavor. Note the guidelines that develop when discipleship is applied in four basic camping concerns:

1. *Camp staffing*. A major emphasis in choosing and training personnel is now the overriding concern for Christian *example*. Discipleship thrives on demonstration.

Cathie Nicoll, longtime Canadian Inter-Varsity camp leader, says it well: "It's what a counselor is that is the most important thing . . . if the counselor is in a relationship with God as he should be and the Holy Spirit has a chance to live and to dominate and permeate . . . God touches the child through the life of the counselor, even beyond what is said."[24]

This involves the total staff. One remembers the Christian camp cook whose temper tantrums in the kitchen made the morning Bible teacher's challenge for joyful living sound rather empty.

The operational implication here is for clear job descriptions for each position. It includes high standards and staff training in understanding and working with campers to effectively teach by life as well as by word.

2. *Camp scheduling.* A key emphasis of this area becomes *flexibility* to encourage an atmosphere of time availability rather than of programs to be run. There is a place for the discipline and orderliness of planned schedules and attention to promptness. However, a discipleship-oriented camp seeks to develop an understanding that the essential focus is on people, not on perfect program.

As indicated by the educational principles of Deuteronomy 6, teaching is not restricted to a scheduled period of time but includes taking advantage of the opportunities provided in daily living (vv. 6-7). How neatly the camping experience fits this prescription for biblical education.

This approach to scheduling is well expressed by Christian camp leader and former American Camping Association president Fred Rogers:

> Our program must create the atmosphere of the camp . . . one where the Holy Spirit can work . . . Are we looking for an atmosphere of precision, efficiency, regimentation, keep busy and rules . . . or is it opportunity for self-expression, through free time, camper planning, some scheduling to create a feeling of security, some opportunity for creative and constructive occupation.[25]

The emphasis on schedule flexibility also has implications for staff time. As a discipler who is alert to taking advantage of both the formal and informal times in the daily schedule, the staff

---

24. Cathie Nicoll, "The Philosophy of the Counselor Centered Camp," *Yearbook of Christian Camping* (North Hollywood, Calif.: Western Conf. and Camp Assoc., 1960), p. 60.

25. Fred Rogers, "What the Church Camp Should Set as Their Goals," *Yearbook of Christian Camping* (North Hollywood, Calif.: Western Conf. and Camp Assoc., 1960), p. 6.

person needs allowance in his personal schedule for the renewal and refreshing that keep his work and testimony sharp. Again, the example of the master Teacher guides us; He made time in the hectic schedule of His day for staff relaxation (Mark 6:31-32).
3. *Camp program.* The discipleship ministry of Christ constantly showed *creativity.* He taught from boats and from the side of mountains; He used the environment for illustrations; He exercised variety in teaching methods. Christian camping should do the same, that is, take the fullest advantage of the camp setting for innovative activities, learning motivation, personal discovery, and productive fellowship.

It is a refreshing experience to visit a camp whose program reflects the camp setting rather than the school gymnasium or Sunday school classroom. There is merit in the determination of one western camp director to avoid at camp all those program activities that could just as well be carried on at the home base.
4. *Camp evangelism.* Evangelism is considered in the discipleship setting as an *ongoing* response to the sincere proclaiming of Christ by word and life in *all* areas of camp living.

The "Follow Me" of Christ's discipling ministry was not an isolated experience. The decision for personal commitment to Him was not restricted to one time or place. Thus, Robert Coleman writes about the evangelistic methods Jesus taught His disciples:

> Evangelism was lived before them in spirit and in technique. . . . He led them to recognize the need inherent in all classes of people, and the best methods of approaching them. They observed how He drew people to Himself. . . . In all types of situations and among all kinds of people, rich and poor, healthy and sick, friend and foe alike, the disciples watched the Master Soul-winner at work. . . . His method was so real and practical that it just came naturally.[26]

What greater opportunity for leading individuals to personal relationship with Jesus Christ than in the discipling setting of the Christian camp? Each staff member shares the privilege of demonstrating the Christian life and each hour of the camp day is available for camper response to the testimony of word and life around him.

Notice also that evangelism in a discipling setting is not the total experience. As stated in the camping purpose, the goal is

26. Robert E. Coleman, *The Master Plan of Evangelism* (Westwood, N.J.: Revell, 1964) pp. 78-79.

Christian maturity. Under the guidance of the Holy Spirit, the Christian camp provides a setting for growing disciples as well as for new ones.

The guidelines we have noted are basic in Christian camping development and indicate the direction a sound camping philosophy provides.[27]

Camp has within it a truly remarkable array of natural attractions and values. In a Christian context it offers the contemporary church one of its richest opportunities toward fulfilling the Savior's directive to make disciples.

As camp and church understand and build together in this perspective, Christian camping moves toward its most productive and satisfying ministry.

---

27. There are contemporary developments in each of these guideline areas. See, for example, Keith Drury "Current Trends in Church Camping," *Journal of Christian Camping*, November-December 1975, pp. 6-7.

SUGGESTIONS FOR STUDY

1. Read and report on some current trends in the camping field as reported in recent magazine articles. If secular camping, indicate any significance for Christian camping.
2. List and evaluate several definitions of camping, besides the ones given in the chapter. What is common to secular and Christian camping? Distinctive?
3. Develop a basic statement on the relationship of church camping to the Sunday school. Indicate how they fit into a total church educational ministry.
4. Illustrate how a Christian education approach to camping provides for camp follow-through.
5. Do you agree or disagree that the church-camping relationship must be a two-way street between the camp professional and the church leader? Why?
6. Obtain and evaluate a local church or denominational statement of camping objectives and/or purpose. How workable is the statement? How would you change it?
7. Apply the overall purpose of Christian camping as stated in the chapter to a Christian camp for the mentally retarded.
8. What is the place of discipleship in a family camp?
9. How would you prepare a camp counselor for a discipling ministry in a high school camp? In a junior camp? In a backpacking camp?
10. Write out six implications of discipleship involved in camp scheduling flexibility.

RESOURCES

American Camping Association. *Camping for American Youth*. Martinsville, Ind.: ACA, 1962.

_____. *Camping IS Education*. Martinsville, Ind.: ACA, 1960.

Davis, Robert Pickens. *Church Camping*. Richmond: John Knox, 1969.

Ensign, John, and Ensign, Ruth. *Camping Together as Christians*. Richmond: John Knox, 1958.

Frank, Doug. "Christian Camping: Philosophy In Action." *Journal of Christian Camping*, August 1970, pp. 5-8.

_____. "Squandered Potential of Christian Camping." *Journal of Christian Camping*, March 1970, pp. 6-8.

Freeberg, William H., and Taylor, Loren E. *Philosophy of Outdoor Education*. Minneapolis: Burgess, 1961.

Johnson, L. Ted. "Conflict . . . Between Change and Continuity." *Journal of Christian Camping*, August 1969, pp. 6-8.

Mattson, Lloyd D. "Wilderness Camping . . . Why?" *Journal of Christian Camping*, April 1969, pp. 5-8.

Mitchell, A. Viola; Robberson, Julia D.; and Obley, June W. *Camp Counseling*. 5th ed. Philadelphia: Saunders, 1977.

National Sunday School Association Camp Commission. *Guiding Principles for Christian Camping*. Chicago: NSSA, 1962.

Pentecost, J. Dwight. *Design for Discipleship*. Grand Rapids: Zondervan, 1971.

Research Report on Christian Camping Activities and Trends. Wheaton, Ill.: Scripture Press, 1970.

Todd, Floyd, and Todd, Pauline. *Camping for Christian Youth*. New York: Harper & Row, 1963.

van der Smissen, Betty. *The Church Camp Program*. Newton, Kans.: Faith and Life, 1961.

2

Camping History

Clifford V. Anderson

CLIFFORD V ANDERSON (Ed. D., Teachers College, Columbia University) is professor of education, Bethel Theological Seminary, St. Paul, Minnesota. Dr. Anderson has been active with Minnesota Baptist Conference camping as program director, leadership class instructor, and member of the state camping committee. He has taught a camping class at Bethel Seminary since 1962.

- *Early Years*
- *Early Leaders*
- *Camping Growth*
- *The Church and Camping*

Camping in the sense of living out-of-doors is as old as mankind. Through the centuries, people have lived close to nature and found there food and shelter.

The Old Testament patriarchs sheltered in tents, their normal habitation (Gen. 12:7-9; 18:1). The Israelites under Moses journeyed from Egypt in a massive, forty-year camping caravan. Israel commemorated this exodus through the Feast of Booths, an annual seven-day family camp-out (Lev. 23:4-43).

John the Baptist was well acquainted with wilderness living (Luke 3:2-6; Mark 1:2-8). Jesus and Paul both spent solitary weeks in the wilderness, meditating on God's will for their lives (Matt. 4:1-11; Gal. 1:15-17).

In primitive societies, camping out was necessitated by the hunt that carried a stalker beyond the range of returning home by nightfall. In some cultures, rites of passage involved an ordeal consisting of going away from the protection of the group to fulfill requirements related to coping with the natural world, thus demonstrating that the child had become a man.

However, to discover the roots of camping as a choice rather than a necessity, we must look beyond nomads, hunters, and primitive peoples.

EARLY YEARS

The beginning of camping as a form of education and recreation may be traced to Greece. The city of Sparta utilized camping for health and fitness, while Athens was concerned with social and aesthetic goals. The Egyptians also made early use of camping.[1] But it is to North America and the United States that we must turn for the most complete story of organized camping. The phenomenon of

---

1. Gerald P. Burns, "A Short History of Camping," *The Camping Magazine*, February 1949, p. 14. H. W. Gibson quotes an article written by Willis Tate, "Is Camping All Greek," in "The History of Organized Camping—Spread of the American Camp to Other Lands," *The Camping Magazine*, December 1936, p. 18, in which the Spartan system of education is compared with methods used in modern organized camps.

camping in the New World has many sources, and evangelism, education, and adventure all contributed.

CAMP MEETINGS

In the western migration away from the settlements of the early American colonies, churches were few and widely spaced. Circuit-riding preachers, farmer-preachers, and teacher-preachers visited and settled among the people moving westward. Outdoor preaching was utilized largely because no adequate buildings existed. In the Virginia Colony, John Waller, a Separate Baptist minister, called his protracted outdoor gatherings *camp meetings*. He set up camp rules around 1775-76.

Methodist circuit riders reached scattered communities and from time to time gathered the "churches" for regional meetings, which were held outdoors since existing buildings could not accommodate the crowds.

The frontier-type camp meeting actually grew out of a religious revival in Kentucky. James McGready, a Presbyterian preacher whose fiery, emotional style aroused opposition to his work in South Carolina, moved to Logan County, Kentucky. Here in 1800 McGready sponsored the first recorded planned camp meeting in America. It was held in July at Gasper River. The people camped in open and covered wagons and in makeshift tents.

The famous Cane Ridge, Kentucky, six-day camp meeting began August 6, 1801, and proved to be the largest outdoor revival in frontier America. Reported attendances ranged from several thousand to twenty-five thousand persons.

As churches and Sunday schools became established, the camp meeting format declined, though some sites continued into the twentieth century as Methodist campgrounds. Others became youth camps, and a few were transformed into middle-class resorts.

The camp meeting had been an effective tool for reaching a widely dispersed and socially and religiously neglected people.[2]

2. For a brief review of the events surrounding the rise of the camp meetings see Howard A. Whaley, "The Second Great Awakening," *Moody Monthly*, January 1976, pp. 40-43. For a recommended book-length treatment of the camp meeting see Charles A. Johnson, *The Frontier Camp Meeting*, Dallas: Southern Methodist U., 1955. Peter Cartwright, *Autobiography of Peter Cartwright*, Nashville: Abingdon, 1956, is a republication of Cartwright's autobiography originally published in 1856 and provides valuable insight into the camp-meeting procedure through which the author was converted and in which he labored for many years in his own style of "muscular Christianity."

CHAUTAUQUA MEETINGS

Like the camp meeting, the Chautauqua movement affected the development of camps and conferences. Here education more or less replaced evangelism as the dominant thrust of the gatherings. The concern of Dr. John H. Vincent, a Methodist clergyman, was to upgrade the work of the Sunday school. His vision of a school of life, teaching all areas of knowledge under the inspiration of Christian commitment, was shared with Lewis Miller, a layman who was a trustee of the Lake Chautauqua Camp Meeting property. In 1874 the first of the famed Chautauqua summer assemblies was held.[3]

In some places the Chautauqua and camp meetings merged activities, but gradually the education and entertainment emphases increased while those of the forest revival declined. With some notable exceptions, the advent of radio, motion pictures, and automobiles ultimately brought an end to the Chautauqua movement.

BIBLE CONFERENCES

More directly related to the denominational and interdenominational camps and conferences of today are the early Bible and missionary conferences. To Dwight L. Moody, the YMCA-trained evangelist, goes the distinction of founding the first Bible conference assembly. After Moody returned from his campaign in England in 1875, he settled at his boyhood home in Northfield, Massachusetts. In 1880 the first summer Northfield Bible Conference was held.

Another widely known Bible conference, which came into existence because of the influence of Northfield, was the Winona gathering at Winona Lake, Indiana. Beginning in 1895, Christians gathered here for emphases similar to those of the Northfield conference. Moody contributed to the work of Winona through sending speakers such as G. Campbell Morgan and F. B. Meyer.[4]

The Mount Herman Association and Conference in California traces its origin to Dr. Hugh W. Gilchrist, a young Seattle pastor who in 1900 had participated in an assembly for Bible study on

---

3. The story of Chautauqua is found in John H. Vincent, *The Chautauqua Movement* (Boston: Chautauqua, 1886). Also see Joseph E. Gould, *The Chautauqua Movement* (Albany: State U. of New York, 1961), and Harry P. Harrison as told to Karl Detzer, *Culture Under Canvas* (New York: Hastings House, 1958).

4. J. William Chapman, *The Life and Work of Dwight L. Moody* (Philadelphia: Winston, 1900), p. 216.

Vashon Island in Puget Sound. In 1905 he directed a similar conference at Glenwood City, California, and at the end of the conference
a vote was taken on the question of whether or not the Pacific Coast
needed a conference ground like Northfield or Winona Lake.
The ballots were unanimous. The property that is now known as
Mt. Hermon was purchased on April 14, 1906.[5]
Today thriving Christian conference centers and camps provide a
full educational program through speakers, classes, and recreational
activities for the whole family. Some are located on old Chautauqua
grounds, others on the sites of former Methodist camp meetings.

OUTDOOR ADVENTURE

From the time of the Pilgrims, who recorded at a meeting on
board their ship, "A small party should go ashore and select a camp
site," accounts of resourcefulness, industry, and adventure in the
outdoors have been part of our American heritage.[6]
Daniel Boone, Davy Crockett, Kit Carson, Henry David
Thoreau, Isaac Walton, "Adirondack" Murray, John Muir, Daniel
Beard, and Earnest Thompson Seton are familiar names in wilderness lore and camping. Another name, though less familiar, is
Hiram Holding, "the founder of modern camping for pleasure." In
1853 he crossed the prairies of America. Later he canoed and
camped in Scotland and Great Britain. Holding wrote the *Campers
Handbook* in 1903, and some consider this the first book on the
general subject.[7]
The camping movement grew rapidly in Europe, especially in
relation to the bicycle and still later the automobile. In 1932 the
Federation-Internationale de Camping et de Caravanning was
formed. This organization is composed of members from many nations, including the camping organizations of the United States and
Canada.
In the United States, camping and hiking were popularized
through the growth of trails in national and state parks. By the late

---

5. Harry A. Smith, *Apart With Him–Fifty Years of the Mount Hermon
   Conference* (Oakland: Western Book and Tract, 1956), p. 9.
6. Lloyd B. Sharp, "The Role of Camping and Our American Heritage,"
   The Camping Magazine, February 1942, p. 11.
7. See the excellent article in *New Encyclopedia Britannica*, 1974, s.v.
   "Camping" for background on the camping movement, especially the
   unorganized form that is considered the fastest growing type of recreation in the world.

1960s more than 135,000 miles of trails served backpackers. More than 450,000 campsites invited the tents of campers.[8]

Private and public campgrounds abound today, as the automobile continues to bring people to the open spaces where they find renewal through recreational camping.

Camping is popular in the wilderness as well as in the resort-type campgrounds having hot water, playgrounds, films, and programs for children. The more than 40 million campers in the United States have spawned a thriving equipment, recreation vehicle, and boating industry.

EARLY LEADERS

Individual initiative played an immensely important role in the founding of institutions such as camping, as the following sketches of early camping leaders show.[9]

FREDRICK WILLIAM GUNN—EDUCATOR

The first organized camp in America was a school-related camp founded by Frederick William Gunn and his wife, Abagail Drinsmede Gunn. They founded and operated a residential school for boys in Washington, Connecticut.

With the advent of the Civil War, boys at the school eagerly played soldier games and camped out from time to time. In the summer of 1861 they hiked to Milford on the Sound, near New Haven, for two happy weeks of boating, sailing, fishing, and tramping. The Gunn camp was part of the school program. It later moved to a lake site where the camps were conducted through the summer of 1897. Gunn is often referred to as the "father of the organized camp."

JOSEPH TRIMBLE ROTHROCK—PHYSICIAN

Dr. Joseph Trimble Rothrock, physician of Wilkes-Barre, Pa.,

---

8. *Encyclopedia Americana International Edition*, 1974, s.v. "Camping."
9. The author is especially indebted to H.W. Gibson for information contained in this section of the chapter. Gibson's articles, eight in all, appeared in *The Camping Magazine*, January—December, 1936. It is unfortunate that his projected book was never published. The Gibson series is the best source of information available on the beginnings of organized camping.

conducted a four-month camp at Lake Gonago for twenty boys. In a biographical sketch he said:

> In 1876 I had the happy idea of taking weakly boys in summer out into camp life in the woods and under competent instruction; mingling exercises and study, so that pursuit of health could be combined with acquisition of practical knowledge outside the usual academic lines. I founded the school of North Mountain, Luzerne County, Pennsylvania, and designated it a School of Physical Culture. There had been, I think, but a single attempt to do this work at an earlier period.[10]

Rothrock thus founded the first private camp. Others guided the health camp in succeeding years. He is also remembered for his efforts in conservation and was called the "father of forestry" in Pennsylvania.

GEORGE W. HINCKLEY—CLERGYMAN

In 1880 Rev. George W. Hinckley, a pastor in West Hartford, Connecticut, took seven boys from his parish on a camping trip to Gardner's Island, Wakefield, Rhode Island. He later established the Goodwill Farm for Boys and the Goodwill Camp at Hinckley, Maine. "The camp took the form of an assembly with a daily program consisting of 'sane and sensible' religious periods, an educational program; swimming, baseball, tennis in the afternoon, and sings, talks and entertainment in the evening."[11] Hinckley found in the Rev. W.H. Murray, or "Adirondack" Murray as he was called, a great example of physical manhood and referred to him as the "father of the modern outdoors movement." Murray wrote in the preface to one of his books:

> To all who camp on shores of lakes, on breezy points, on banks of rivers, by shady beaches, on slopes of mountains, and under green trees anywhere, I, an old camper, a wood lover, an aboriginal veneered with civilization, send greeting. I thank God for the multitude of you; for the strength and the beauty of you; for the healthfulness of your tastes and the naturalness of your natures. I eat and drink with you; I hunt and fish with you; I boat and bathe with you; and with you day and night enjoy the gifts of the good world.[12]

---

10. Joseph T. Rothrock, quoted by H.W. Gibson, "The History of Organized Camping—The Early Days," *The Camping Magazine*, January 1936, p. 15.

11. Ibid, p. 26.

12. Ibid.

ERNEST BERKELEY BALCH—COLLEGE STUDENT

Ernest Berkeley Balch's inspiration for starting a boys' camp grew out of his reaction to the plight of sons of the well-to-do who were boarded in summer hotels with their families. The idea for a camp emerged during his sophomore year at Dartmouth. In the summer of 1881 he located a perfect site on Burnt Island at Big Asquam Wilderness, New Hampshire, and started Camp Chocorua. This pioneering camp did not pamper boys with staff that cooked and cleaned. Campers were organized in small groups under boy leadership and did the work in the camp as well as having special activities and fun. Balch opposed mass camping and regimented schedules. As camps later multiplied, he and others associated with Camp Chocorua scorned the out-of-doors-boarding-home style that characterized them.[13]

Reports from the Balch camp showed creativity that continues to influence the camping movement. The division of labor, achievement tests, staff training, and group work have greatly affected the educational philosophy of camping.

SUMNER F. DUDLEY—BUSINESSMAN AND YMCA WORKER

In the August 1, 1885 issue of *The Watchman*, Sumner F. Dudley wrote, "I have just returned from eight days in camp, conscious of having one of the most profitable times of my life; with me have been seven of the leading members of the Boy's Branch of Newburgh."[14] Camp Bald Head, as it was called because the boys had their hair cut short before going to camp, was located at Orange Lake near Newburgh, New York. Dudley repeated the experience the following year with twenty-three boys at Lake Wawayanda, New Jersey. His experience with boys and camping led him to leave his surgical instrument manufacturing and enter the work of the YMCA in 1887. In 1891 there were eighty-three campers at Lake Champlain near Westport, New York. Camp Dudley is the oldest existing camp and was the first of the organizational camps. A worldwide camping movement through the YMCA was built upon the beginning made by Sumner F. Dudley.[15]

---

13. Julian H. Salomon, "A Diamond Jubilee for Camping," *The Camping Magazine*, December 1956, p. 26.
14. H.W. Gibson, "The History of Organized Camping—Establishment of Institutional Camps," *The Camping Magazine*, March 1936, p. 18.
15. Ibid.

ERNEST THOMPSON SETON AND ROBERT BADEN-POWELL

Robert Baden-Powell developed Scouting as a branch of army training while serving in the British army in 1876. In 1907 he set up a trial camp on Brownsea Island in England, and in 1908 he issued *Scouting for Boys*. Ernest Thompson Seton headed the committee that organized the Boy Scouts of America in 1910. He wrote the handbook *Boy Scouts of America* (1910) in which his remarks on camping dealt more with camping trips than organized camping.

The national Boy Scout movement popularized camping. "It put the spotlight on camping as a character-influencing factor, as an education for living, and therefore, as an ally in the work of the home, the school, the church."[16]

DR. AND MRS. LUTHER HALSEY GULICK

While the Philadelphia YMCA had in Asbury Park, New Jersey, a summer boarding and vacation house for tired young women earning their own living in 1874, the first camp for girls was begun by Mr. and Mrs. Luther Halsey Gulick for their daughter and her friends in 1888 on the Thames River in Connecticut.[17] The Gulicks later established Camp Sebago-Wohelo in Maine in 1910 and founded the organization known as Camp Fire Girls, chartered in 1912.

H.W. GIBSON

H.W. Gibson, a chronicler of the history of organized camping, made many contributions to the movement. He founded Camp Becket in 1903 and had an active role in the first camping convention in Boston the same year. He wrote the first book on organized camping, *Camping for Boys*, in 1911. In 1927 he founded a camp for girls and was president of the Camp Directors Association. He also was the first editor of its magazine.[18]

---

16. William D. Murray, *The History of the Boy Scouts of America* (New York: BSA, 1937), p. 422.
17. Robert E. McBride, *Camping at the Mid-Century* (Chicago: ACA, 1953), p. 2.
18. The May 1941 *Camping Magazine* article, "H. W. Gibson," p. 11, notes some of his contributions.

Camping Growth

FROM NEW ENGLAND TO THE CONTINENT

Organized camping was born in New England, but it did not take long to extend south and west. In 1898 the first camp in the South was established. Camping began "out west" with a Michigan camp in 1904. Camp Indianola opened in Wisconsin in 1907 and Camp Mishawaka in Minnesota in 1909. According to statistics compiled by Porter Sargent in 1933, there was an increase in camps of 491 percent from 1915 to 1924 and of 179 percent from 1924 to 1933. There were 211 camps listed in 1915 and 3,485 in 1933. In 1923, 90 percent of all camps were in New England. By 1933, New England had 618 private camps, New York 236, California 56, Colorado 32, and Minnesota and Iowa 10 each.[19]

The growth of camping was at the private and organizational levels. Private camps were frequently founded by educators and were operated as a summer experiential educational effort and business, as well as a service to interested families. Organizational camps were part of the year-round youth-serving programs of the sponsoring organizations.

Boy Scout, Girl Scout, and YMCA camps experienced dramatic growth during this period and continue to play a major role in the camping movement in America.

Along with camping growth, agency camps introduced camping innovations. The Boston YMCA conducted a camp school for boys in tents on Commonwealth Avenue in the city in 1909. The school continued from July 7 through August 25. Mornings were devoted to classes and afternoons to recreational activities. The boys went to their homes at night. This was probably the first day camp.

The American Camping Association's "1966 Fact Sheet" reported approximately 8,000 resident camps: 3,048 for boys; 2,232 for girls; and 2,720 coed. There were approximately 3,200 day camps.

> In 1920 there were approximately 2,000 resident camps only
> In 1940 there were approximately 4,399 resident camps only
> In 1950 there were approximately 6,032 resident and day camps
> In 1960 there were approximately 10,039 resident and day camps
> In 1965 there were approximately 11,200 resident and day camps[20]

A national camping survey made for the summer of 1968 esti-

---

19. H.W. Gibson, "The History of Organized Camping—The Private Camps," *The Camping Magazine*, April 1936, p. 18.
20. "1966 Fact Sheet" (Martinsville, Indiana: ACA), pp. 1-2.

mated there were at that time 10,682 camps with 7,796,333 campers. Of these, 1,348,487 were disadvantaged.[21]
In 1974 the ACA reported a total of 2,964 affiliated camps, 928 of which were private, 150 undesignated, and the remainder organizational camps. These included 328 Protestant, 81 Catholic, and 29 Jewish camps. An unofficial estimate of total camps operating in 1975 put the number between ten and twelve thousand.[22] This included organized day camps. In 1977 about three thousand camps were affiliated with the American Camping Association. Developing accurate statistics is difficult. Should retreats and caravans be considered camps? How many days duration constitutes a camp? Definitions as well as inadequate communication contribute to the lack of precision.

CAMPING WORLDWIDE

In 1911 the American camping movement was carried around the world by the YMCA. Camps were established in lands where YMCA work was being done. The first international boys' camp took place in 1924 in Switzerland under sponsorship of the World Committee of the YMCA, as documented by Gibson.[23]
Scouting Jamborees also attracted world attention. In 1933, 30,000 boys from thirty-seven nations participated in the gathering in Godollo, Hungary.
Private camps, organizational camps, and church-related camps abroad were often begun by individuals who had contact with camping in the United States or Canada. It is now common to find camps in countries where American missionaries labor. International partnership exists between some camps overseas and camping organizations in America.
The impact of camping on youth can be illustrated by the use made of the camp by the Soviet Union. It has been reported that each summer 70 percent of Soviet youth ten to fifteen years of age

21. "National Camping Survey," Battelle Memorial Institute, September 1968, American Camping Association received this report.
22. Correspondence and telephone interviews with Eleanor P. Eels, former Director of the Fund for the Advancement for Camping, and with the office of the American Camping Association.
23. H. W. Gibson, "The History of Organized Camping—Spread of the American Camp to Other Lands," The Camping Magazine, December 1936, p. 18.

attend a twenty-six-day camp where enthusiasm for the Communist way of life is instilled.[24]

Individual camp-outs and family camping, as distinguished from organized camping, is also a worldwide phenomenon. In the 1970s it is estimated that 60 million camping enthusiasts take to the countryside yearly—half of them from North America and most of the rest from European countries.[25]

Canada reports a vigorous camping movement and a growing number of effective Christian camps and conferences throughout the provinces.

As camping grew, the need was recognized for an organization that could provide a basis for fellowship among camp leaders and help set standards. Dr. Winthrop M. Talbot, director of Camp Asquam, in an address delivered at a New York conference in 1902, called for such an association. Under Talbot's leadership, the first camp conference was held in Boston, April 15-17, 1903. About one hundred men and several women attended. A loose organization known as the General Camp Association was formed. This became the American Camping Association at its Cleveland convention in 1935.

In 1920, Teachers College, Columbia University, offered the first course for camp leaders, and five years later Laura Matoon introduced the first counselor training program at Camp Kehonka.[26]

The Church and Camping

THE EARLY YEARS

We have already referred to George W. Hinkley's church camp in 1880. Late in the nineteenth century and early in the twentieth, some urban churches sponsored fresh-air houses, farms, and vacations especially for poor children of the cities.

The first Catholic camp was established in 1892 by St. Ann's Academy of Lake Champlain, New York.

Generally, however, churches and denominations were slow to enter the camping field. This may have been due partly to the Christian leadership and religious nature of many of the existing

---

24. Robert W. Harlan, "Camping in Russia," *The Camping Magazine*, May 1963, p. 16.

25. *New Encyclopedia Britannica*, s.v. "Camping."

26. H.W. Gibson, "The History of Organized Camping, Leadership Training Conference and Courses," *The Camping Magazine*, November 1936.

organizational and private camps; the churches perhaps felt there was little need for them to develop camps.

The International Sunday School Association (later the International Council of Religious Education) conducted an interdenominational summer program at Lake Geneva, Wisconsin, in 1914. This is sometimes referred to as the origin of the church camping movement.[27]

The earliest church camps were really assemblies for youth and young adults; they followed the general format of the adult Bible conference. Large group meetings were held several times a day. In addition some recreation and informal group activities were planned.

Church camps pioneered coed camps for youth. "The movement spread like wildfire—at last the churches had found something that 'clicked' with the early adolescent boy and girl."[28]

LATER GROWTH

In 1938 the Committee on Religious Education of Children of the International Council of Religious Education appointed a subcommittee to study the situation regarding children's attendance at camp. A *Manual for Guidance for Junior Camps Under Church Auspices, and Religious Emphasis in Junior Camps* was published in 1939. In a later revision the Committee reported:

> In the years since 1939, however, the trend toward junior camping has grown by leaps and bounds. Many denominations report thousands of junior children attending church-sponsored camps for their age group. The movement has increased more rapidly than adequate leadership and programs have been developed. As a result many junior camps are mere downward extensions of youth conferences and fail to meet the basic needs of junior children.[29]

In 1942 the International Council of Religious Education published *Planning the Family Camp* and in 1950 a manual of camping standards for church camping entitled *Toward Better Church Camping*. The appearance of a pamphlet by Reynold E. Carlson, *Day Camping for Your Church*, published by Judson Press in 1948, was an indication of church interest and activity in this type of camping.

27. Elizabeth Brown, "Camps and Summer Conferences," in *Orientation in Religious Education*, ed. Philip Henry Lotz (Nashville: Abingdon-Cokesbury, 1950), p. 340.
28. Ibid., p. 341.
29. Committee on Religious Education of Children, *A Manual for Leaders of Church Camps for Junior Boys and Girls* (Chicago: International Council of Religious Education, 1947), p. 3.

The famed Southern Baptist Ridgecrest Baptist Conference Center in North Carolina was started in 1909 by Bernard W. Spilman, an employee of the Baptist Sunday School Board. In addition to this year-round conference center, the denomination also conducts resident camps for boys and girls.

Glorietta, New Mexico, is another national conference center for Southern Baptists. The Southern Baptist Convention through its Sunday School Board has extensive resources for resident and day camping and church recreation. At this writing there are 601 Southern Baptist Camps or assemblies. These are part of the ministry of local, county, or state associations.[30]

The Green Lake Center of the national American Baptist Assembly at Green Lake, Wisconsin, had its first season in 1944. Annual attendance now reaches fifty-thousand persons with over four hundred groups scheduled. Green Lake has added family camping to its conference schedule.

The camping history of the Baptist General Conference is probably similar to that of other small evangelical groups. The Chicago Young People's Union had its first summer assembly in 1924 at Bethany Beach, Michigan. In 1925 the Minnesota Youth met at Bethel College and Seminary, and in succeeding years the state denomination purchased land and established Trout Lake Camp. Other districts followed, either purchasing camping properties and developing facilities or renting campsites.

The National Council of Churches has had a committee on camps and conferences since 1946. It is now known as the Committee on Outdoor Education.

The National Sunday School Association, a National Association of Evangelicals-related education agency that was especially strong in the forties through the sixties, formed a Camp Commission in 1959. In 1962 NSSA published study papers on philosophy and resources for church camps.[31]

CURRENT DEVELOPMENTS

Church camping is related to the American Camping Association through the Committee on Outdoor Education of the National

---

30. A list of these camps was provided June 10, 1976 by the office of John LaNoue of the Church Recreation Department of the Sunday School Board of the Southern Baptist Convention.

31. Philosophy Committee, National Sunday School Association Camp Commission, *Guiding Principles for Church Camping, and Evangelical Camp Resources* (Chicago: NSSA, 1962).

Council of Churches and through direct participation in ACA national and regional sections. The ACA sponsors a church camping committee.

Christian Camping International now serves as the professional organization for conservative, evangelical Christian camps and conferences. The Western Camp and Conference Association had formed a loose organization that attracted participants from other areas. It eventually became in 1959 the Christian Camps and Conferences Association. In 1963 CCCA became an international organization that in 1968 took the name *Christian Camping International*.

Graham Tinning, executive director of the Western Camps and Conference Association was chosen to be the first executive of the merged groups. He served until his death in 1968, when he was succeeded by Edward Ouland.

Like the American Camping Association, CCI serves its members and the camping movement through research, publications, leadership training programs, conventions, and opportunities for fellowship and interaction among camp leaders.

SUGGESTIONS FOR STUDY

1. Where and to what purpose was camping found in the ancient world?
2. Research one of the historic camp meetings. Report on family living conditions, program features, and the social and religious significance of the camp meeting.
3. Trace the origins of the Chautauqua movement. Describe its program and influence.
4. What role did the Bible conference play in the development of Christian camping?
5. Report the motivations that led early leaders to establish the first camps.
6. What special significance was assigned to camping in the Scouting movement?
7. Describe the growth of camping in North America and worldwide. List factors you feel contributed to this growth.
8. What reasons can you list for the relatively late entry of the Christian church into the field of youth camping?
9. Report on the structure and objectives of the American Camping Association.
10. Research the history of Christian Camping International and prepare a résumé of its purpose, services, and current membership.

RESOURCES

Bibliographic material is contained in the extensive footnotes.

3

Forms of Camping

Lloyd D. Mattson

- *The Centralized Camping Approach*
- *The Decentralized Camping Approach*
- *The Eclectic Camping Approach*
- *Major Types of Camping*

The student of contemporary camping will discover that Christian camping has a wide variety of forms. There are camps that stay on one site for the whole camp period, and there are camps that move to a new site every day. There are camps that emphasize large group meetings and other camps that work almost entirely with small

LLOYD D. MATTSON (B.A., John Wesley College) is pastor of North Shore Baptist Church, Duluth, Minnesota. He has been director of camping, Baptist General Conference; director, Pine Lake Baptist camp (Iowa); editor, *Journal of Christian Camping*; and author of camping publications, including *Camping Guideposts, Family Camping*, and *Wilderness Way*.

groups. There are camps for all ages. This chapter will provide a basis for classifying the major forms of camping.

The two broadest *divisions* of camping are *informal* and *organized*. According to its simplest, informal definition, camping is outdoor living. However, when there is also group living and programming to meet specific objectives under trained leadership, such outdoor living is considered organized camping.

Camping is further identified by its *sponsorship* category. Two major categories here would be *general* and *religious* or, for the purpose of this text, *Christian*. The specific sponsors could be individuals, or organizations such as social agencies, schools, denominations, churches.

There are three other ways to classify camps. The *type* of camp relates to its physical conditions. A *resident* camp has a permanent campsite; the campers spend a major portion of their time on the site. The *nonresident* camp does not include lodging on consecutive nights at a permanent site. Trip, travel (mobile), and day camps represent this type.

Camps are further identified by *age groups* ranging from children to full family groupings. Finally, camps may also be classified in terms of *special interests*. Here we have camps for the handicapped, music camps, sport camps, and camps for other specific emphases.

Thus there may be a Christian organized residential camp for mentally handicapped children. It is identified by the kind of sponsorship, physical condition, special interest, and age group.

Before discussing the specific types of Christian camping, it will be helpful to consider a major factor in camping form—the camp approach. There are three main approaches in organized camping, and each has its particular influence on such areas as program, staff responsibilities, and facility development. The approaches can be identified by the terms *centralized* and *decentralized* plus a third category, *eclectic*.

A camping approach—the underlying emphasis—is determined by both history and philosophy. The stages through which camping has come, as outlined in chapter 2, for example, are reflected in how camps today operate. The purpose and objectives of a camp likewise effect organization and methodology.

In its purest form, the *centralized camping approach* focuses mainly on large-group activity; minimal initiatives are required from cabin unit leaders. It seeks to fulfill the camping purpose mainly through preaching and teaching in all-camp meetings. The remaining parts of the camp program, while not discounted as to physical values, are not seen as primarily involved in fulfilling the spiritual purpose of the camp.

Leaders are trained and the camp program designed to create the best possible climate for effective all-camp programs of Bible teaching, evangelism, missionary education, and challenges to life commitment. The primary method of communication is the sermonic message. Outstanding speakers are recruited and strong support programs of music are used. The public evangelistic invitation often is prominent following chapel or campfire services, and preparation is made to counsel campers who respond.

In contrast to the centralized emphasis, the *decentralized camping approach* focuses on the cabin unit led by a capable counselor. The program here is designed to provide maximum involvement in small-group activity. The understanding is that the camp purpose of discipling campers will be achieved most directly through the personal influence of the counselor.

Cabin unit leaders are carefully selected and trained to lead campers in a variety of adventure experiences to allow opportunity for personal counseling. In its purest form, the camper would rarely assemble with the entire camp body, except as necessary for activities such as meals, awards-giving, or orientation.

Neither centralized nor decentralized camping in its absolute form is normally found in resident camping, for practical considerations render this all but impossible. Yet the distinct influence of these approaches will be observed when today's forms of Christian camping are explored. Let us therefore examine these approaches in more depth.

The Centralized Camping Approach

HISTORY

Useful illustrations for understanding the differences between centralized and decentralized approaches to camping can be found in most churches. The graded Sunday school, for example, is a decentralized approach to Bible teaching. The Sunday morning worship is a centralized emphasis. The values in both approaches are evident. The degree of effectiveness in communication rests largely on the skills of the teacher or preacher.

Chapter 2 noted that early Christian camping was little more than a transplant of the church service from indoors to outdoors. It is not surprising, therefore, that a centralized approach prevailed. The congregation attending to the preacher has usually been a norm for major Christian communication throughout church history.

The development from camp meeting to Bible conference to youth assembly was quite natural, and little occasion arose to question the communication approach used. Multiplied thousands, young and old, bear testimony to the spiritual values found in these assemblies and the sawdust trails of historic encampments.

Because of traditions held in common with the early fathers of organized Christian camping, it was natural that denominational camps followed the centralized approach to programming. Since the leaders often were clergymen, the chapel service became the most promising focal point for spiritual input.

EMPHASIS

As already noted, the centralized approach emphasizes the all-camp meeting. Several programs each day may be offered in the chapel or outdoor meeting place. Frequently Bible teachers will instruct smaller groups, but the counselor normally does not have Bible teaching responsibility. He is usually expected to be alert for opportunities to reinforce the spiritual impressions a camper may gain through the preaching.

Recreation often is guided by program specialists while campers choose among several activities to fill the hours between meals and meetings. Instruction may be offered in swimming, boating, crafts, sports, and games, though campers usually do not participate as cabin groups.

The dormitory housing once common to camps following the centralized approach is yielding to cabin-unit housing, as awareness of the benefits gained by the smaller group has grown. But the sleeping hours and possibly the afternoon rest period may be the only time cabin mates spend with their counselor. Cabin devotions led by the counselor prior to bedtime are encouraged.

ADVANTAGES

The advantages of the centralized approach are reflected in the history of camp staffing. In the early years professional camp leadership was nearly nonexistent. Leadership fell to the ministers who were forced to recruit untrained volunteers to staff the camps.

Lacking trained or experienced personnel to deal with campers about spiritual matters, camps prudently followed the familiar pattern of the home church. History records the blessing that fell on the Bible conference and youth assemblies of yesterday, and the blessings continue where dedicated Christians preach and teach God's Word to campers.

DISADVANTAGES

The disadvantages of centralized camping appear when one considers the rich potential of the camp setting for the camper. Often little is made of the natural surroundings. Recreation may follow the pattern of the playground and feature team sports that satisfy those with athletic skill.

Little opportunity is provided in this approach for the counselor to share in Bible study with his or her cabin unit. The point of contact for spiritual concerns is largely that gained by being in the same meeting. Since the cabin group rarely meets together, apart from sleeping, opportunities for counselor-camper contacts are reduced.

Many skills and learning experiences not usually possible at home are lost to the camper when large-group activity is featured. Craft programs often parallel those the camper has already had in vacation Bible school, and the world of nature crafts remains undiscovered.

Where the emphasis is placed on chapel attendance, program features such as extended hikes or camp-outs are generally bypassed. The potential spiritual impact of a cabin group sitting around a campfire in the outpost camp is missed.

While campers involved in this approach may get to know a greater number of fellow campers, the closer friendships that grow when a small group spends much time together often do not occur.

INFLUENCE ON THE CAMPSITE

The approach a camp selects for its program will of necessity influence the development of the camp property. The chapel becomes the focal point of the camp. Often having a capacity much greater than required for youth camps, it provides for occasional rallies and adult conferences.

Housing in dormitories is a logical solution to group control with minimum staff. Frequently camp buildings were clustered as close together as possible to provide ready access to the chapel and dining hall.

Sometimes prime forest was swept away to clear space for the athletic field and ball diamond. Limited thought was given to the aesthetic values of the natural setting or to the harmony of architecture with the surroundings.

As years have passed it has become evident that even the staunchest proponents of the centralized approach have become aware of the need to reevaluate how well the potential of the camping experience is actually being utilized.

THE DECENTRALIZED CAMPING APPROACH

HISTORY

It has been stated that neither the centralized nor the decentralized approach to camping is practiced in its absolute form. That it is a matter of emphasis will be noticed as we examine the decentralized approach.

From the beginning, private secular camping was largely organized in a decentralized pattern because this suited its educational-recreational purpose. Summer camp was a place for city-bound youth to escape to the country for a six- to eight-week vacation. Here they enjoyed recreation and instruction under the supervision of program specialists. The campers were supervised by counselors who were assigned to their living units. Each living unit, functioning independently of the others, followed a schedule arranged by the camp and was led by the counselor. Except for meals, the whole camp seldom gathered together.

Agency camps such as those sponsored by the Scouts and the YMCA followed this approach. It was in these camps that many Christian young people first experienced camping. Later participating in church camping programs, they brought with them some of the program ideas common to agency camps. Viewed at times with suspicion, decentralized innovations such as cookouts, horseback riding, outpost camping, and nature crafts were gradually accepted and found a place in many Christian camping programs.

The growth of the independent Christian camp and agency camps such as Christian Service Brigade, Pioneer Girls, and Awana also influenced the forms of church-related camping. With programs suited to the objectives of the sponsoring agencies, the decentralized approach was usually followed. As leaders experienced in this kind of camping served in the more traditional camps, new program ideas were introduced there. Campers, too, influenced the form, for the appeal of more adventuresome programs could not be denied, and denominational camp leaders recognized that the felt needs of the camper had to be reckoned with if he were to be attracted to camp.

Many Christian camps today are organized after the decentralized approach while sharing the spiritual purpose of those Christian camps that continue in the centralized pattern.

In decentralized camping, emphasis is placed on the cabin unit under the careful guidance of a trained, dedicated counselor. Deliberate effort is made to create maximum opportunity for the counselor to work with his or her cabin group.

The counselor has the primary responsibility for Bible teaching and devotional guidance and for guiding the camper toward spiritual growth.

Usually the activity and craft program centers in the camp setting rather than in the things a camper experiences regularly at home. While the staff may include program specialists, most activities will be shared by the cabin unit.

Meals are usually taken in the dining hall where the cabin group is seated together. Occasionally there will be cookouts and campouts as cabin groups leave the camp for an extended period for adventure and spiritual discovery.

A general rule for decentralized camping is: whatever can be done by the cabin unit together will be done that way. Confidence is placed in the counselor for the spiritual and physical well-being of each camper in his group.

ADVANTAGES

A practical advantage in the decentralized approach is the broadening of program potential for the individual camper. Each cabin unit can adopt a schedule of activities that suits its interests. Since time is more flexible, a greater variety of experiences can be gained.

The counselor, given more time to become acquainted with each camper in his group, is thus allowed greater opportunity to influence the camper for Christ on a personal basis.

Campers become better acquainted with other campers in the cabin. This provides opportunity for a greater influence of camper on camper and for lasting friendships to grow. Timid campers may find greater security as friendships develop.

Group control is potentially more effective, as each counselor is responsible for his few campers. More attention can be given each camper. Personal needs may be discovered and met.

DISADVANTAGES

An obvious difficulty with decentralized camping lies in the challenge of assuring each cabin unit a capable, dedicated counselor. The program needs such capable leaders to achieve fully its purposes. Camps relying on one-week volunteers sometimes have problems finding enough qualified people to take fullest advantage of the decentralized approach. (Of considerable potential help here is the development of a course on camp counseling by Moody Correspondence School.[1]

Lacking a good counselor, a camp experience where the counselor is emphasized may have a negative influence on campers. The modeling of life before campers, acclaimed as the strength of decentralized camping, also has effect when the modeling is weak. Poor counselors, of course, have a negative effect in any camping situation. (For more on this, see the section on counselors in chapter 8.)

Camps with severe facility limitations might find the decentralized approach difficult to implement. If buildings and grounds provide for little more than team sports and meetings, an action-adventure program for small groups might have problems.

INFLUENCE ON THE CAMPSITE

Since the focal point is the small group, decentralized camping has little need for large assembly buildings or areas. Space between housing units is desirable to allow greater seclusion and fewer distractions for the cabin groups.

The emphasis on nature-related activity calls for the preservation of the natural setting to the highest practical degree. Small activity centers scattered throughout the camp make unnecessary the acres of clearing needed for field sports.

Since architecture is designed for minimum intrusion by buildings and roads, the natural landscape is retained. Buildings are set back from the lake to preserve the beauty of the shoreline. As many opportunities as possible are sought by campsite planners to expose campers to the wonders and joys of the natural world.

---

1. Werner C. Graendorf and Jerry Crosby, *Christian Camp Counseling Correspondence Course* (Chicago: Moody, 1979).

THE ECLECTIC CAMPING APPROACH

Observation of current camping practice indicates that neither of the two approaches discussed is widely practiced in totality. Camp leaders are reasonable people, and while a person may feel more comfortable with a bias toward one position or the other, most often a blending of the two will be found. Values of traditional camping are retained, and rewarding features from newer approaches are added. We have called this the *eclectic* camping approach, since *eclectic* means "selecting and using the best elements." This appears to be a basic trend in camping form.

Thus, the typical Christian youth camp today will probably feature some all-camp activity, but the counselors will be expected to be with their cabin groups. Though there may be one or more all-camp worship service each day, the counselors will be assigned Bible teaching and devotional responsibility as well.

A vital factor in this approach is the trend toward providing more thorough and effective training for counselors, both salaried and volunteer. The position of the counselor has steadily gained stature, and more now recognize him as a key person in the camp ministry.

The eclectic approach to camping thus recognizes value in all-camp activity, while emphasizing the discipling importance of the counselor working with individuals in the cabin group. This blend of old and newer approaches to Christian camping offers the camp a versatility denied when either basic form is slavishly pursued.

MAJOR TYPES OF CAMPING

RESIDENT CAMPING

For the foreseeable future the resident youth camp probably will continue to be the basic type of camp and serve the greatest number of campers.

It should be noted, however, that camping has spread far beyond the traditional resident program. The use of the resident camp to serve special purposes and interests continues to find new expressions, as is noted in chapter 7.

Resident youth camps usually take children above grade three. Younger boys and girls find day camp more appealing than the extended absence from home and parents that resident camping requires.

Christian camps divide campers into grade groupings paralleling the Sunday school: juniors—grades four through six; junior high—

grades seven, eight, (nine)*; and high school—grades (nine), ten, eleven, and twelve.

Some camps concentrate on a ministry to one age group. These camps develop a facility and program geared to the interest of the grades they serve. For example, Camp Ha-Lu-Wa-Sa in New Jersey, serving juniors, houses them in a "frontier village" facility. An island fort provides overnight adventure, and a two-mile narrow-gauge railroad adds further attraction.

On the other hand, in the same camp junior high youth may enjoy a teepee camp, while high school youth are served through bike, canoe, and backpack trips.

Many Christian camps are coed through all grades, although some camps continue to offer separate boys and girls programs through junior high years.

While this book is concerned with camping, it should be noted that the Bible conference movement is very active. Thousands of persons of all ages attend conferences throughout the summer in many parts of the United States and Canada. Bible conferences appeal to families, and while the program often is designed particularly for adults, special features may be planned for children and youth.

Resident camping reaches beyond boys and girls to meet the needs of many kinds of persons and to fulfill specialized interests. These will be discussed in detail in chapter 7. Family camps gain in popularity year after year. Camps for disadvantaged and handicapped persons, for senior adults, and for other special groupings demonstrate the versatility of the camping idea.

The normal camping time schedule is in one-week periods. However, the short-term camp, usually known as a *retreat*, has been an important part of Christian camping. Usually conducted on a weekend basis, retreats serve many age and interest groupings. These include men's groups, women's groups, couples, single adults, college-career, senior adults, choirs, and church boards.

Camps with proper facilities and proximity to population centers provide a year-round opportunity to minister through weekend and holiday retreats.

NONRESIDENT CAMPING

While the traditional resident camp continues to be camping's basic form, nonresident kinds of programs are mushrooming.

Day camp. The popular day camp serves many thousands of

---

*Niner camps, concentrating on that vital, transitional grade, are becoming increasingly common.

younger boys and girls each summer, and in some areas the values of day camping are being enjoyed by senior adults as well. Having no need for overnight accommodations, day camping can be offered almost anywhere controlled, open space is available.

Nonresident camping programs are largely mobile. Participants move daily or frequently from one camping place to another. While standard nomenclature is still being developed, the following definitions for mobile types of camping are generally acceptable.

Travel camp. Travel camping is a motorized mobile camp, where campers travel via buses, cars, or possibly motorcycles. The group may visit sites of special interest to fulfill program objectives.

A family camping caravan would be a form of travel camp. The missionary caravan, where youth serve a mission purpose accessible by road, camping as they go, would be another form.

Trip camping. This term refers to nonmotorized mobile camping. Travel may be by means of bicycle, horseback, canoe, kayak, or other watercraft powered by human energy, and hiking.

In a day when the isolated wilderness is becoming increasingly scarce, many trip camps must follow back roads and well-traveled waterways. Groups may camp in public or private campgrounds.

The ideal of a true wilderness, however, continues to lure thousands each year, and among them are many tripping groups sponsored by Christian camps. The wilderness canoe route or the mountain and forest trail offer many values to campers. Here the camper confronts nature with his home, food, and shelter in his pack. Two general types of wilderness camp may be identified: the *wilderness trail camp* and the *wilderness stress camp*.

The trail camp seeks to involve the camper in basic wilderness living through allowing him to practice outdoor-living skills. One objective is to learn how to live comfortably with minimal provisions under all conditions in the wilderness.

Stress camping utilizes the wilderness as a testing place. Deliberate hardships are sought out or created to pit the person against nature. Advanced wilderness skills such as rock climbing, rappelling, whitewater canoeing, or kayaking form parts of many stress programs. Forced marches, extended periods of isolation with only the barest necessities for safety (often called the *solo*), become testing experiences. This type of trip camping demands a careful conditioning of the camper and highest leadership skills of supervisors.

The student of trip camping will recognize that camping programs are highly individualistic and employ a blending of approaches and forms. Just as resident camping has evolved from varying traditions, so trip camping assumes ecletic patterns, each with its champions.

SUGGESTIONS FOR STUDY

1. Write a description of a centralized camp and list the strengths of this approach.
2. List several influences that brought about change in centralized Christian youth camps.
3. Contrast the role of the cabin counselor in the centralized and decentralized approaches to Christian camping.
4. Describe the differences one might expect in campsite development to serve the program needs of centralized and decentralized camping.
5. Identify the disadvantages found in centralized and decentralized Christian camping.
6. What benefits can be gained by adopting the eclectic approach to camping?
7. How does the campsite influence the camping program?
8. Plan a summer camp schedule that would serve a group of thirty medium-sized churches, allowing at least one week of camp for each person from grade three through twelve. You have ten weeks available. Defend your choice of age and sex groupings.
9. Write out the differences between resident and nonresident camping and identify several types of each.
10. List the basic program difference between wilderness trail camping and wilderness stress camping.

RESOURCES

Bell, Arvine. "A Philosophy Statement for Camps Ridgecrest and Crestridge." *Journal of Christian Camping,* July-August 1972, pp. 8-10.

Davis, Robert Pickens. *Church Camping.* Richmond: John Knox, 1969.

Dimock, Hedley S. *Administration of the Modern Camp.* New York: Association, 1957.

Frank, Doug. "Toward a Philosophy of Christian Camping." *Journal of Christian Camping,* May 1970, pp. 6-8.

Hanelius, Ray. "The Deerfoot Lodge Camping Philosophy Determines the Basic Program." *Journal of Christian Camping,* July-August 1976, p. 4.

Klein, Mary Anne. "Flexibility and Freedom: A New Approach to Camping." *Journal of Christian Camping,* March-April 1977, pp. 7-9.

Mattson, Lloyd D. *Camping Guideposts.* Chicago: Moody, 1972.

————. *The Wilderness Way.* Cotton, Minn.: Whiteface Woods, 1970.

Mitchell, A. Viola; Crawford, Ida B.; and Robberson, Julia D. *Camp Counseling.* 4th ed. Philadelphia: Saunders, 1970.

Nicoll, Cathie. "Life and Ministry." *Journal of Christian Camping,* January-February 1977, pp. 11-14.

Todd, Floyd, and Todd, Pauline. *Camping for Christian Youth.* New York: Harper & Row, 1963.

van der Smissen, Betty. *The Church Camp Program, Its Planning And Development.* Newton, Kans.: Faith and Life, 1961.

H. Wright, Norman. *Help! I'm a Camp Counselor.* Glendale, Calif.: Regal, 1968.

Unit 2

Christian Camping Program

What do you do in a Christian camp? And just as important, why do you do it?

Before setting up the camp program, which will answer the first question, it is recommended that consideration be given the second question which relates to understanding what lies behind the program that is being developed. Thus there are *two* chapters on camp program.

The first chapter discusses *program principles* and spells out some of the underlying considerations that go into program planning for a Christian camp. It is designed to make programming a great deal more than mere time filling.

The follow-up chapter, dealing with *program activities*, gets into program material under the headings of spiritual, physical, social, and recreational. There are helpful program ideas and resources.

Chapter 6 is an expansion of the brief reference to crafts in the activities chapter. It is a thorough presentation of the place of *arts and crafts* in Christian camp.

The setting for the program discussed here is essentially the resident camp—permanent facilities, campers remaining on site, and normal children-youth orientation. However, there are an increasing number of variations in both resident and nonresident type camping. These represent *specialized programs* to meet specialized needs and interests, as discussed in chapter 7.

While certain fundamental program principles can be applied to almost any type of camping, it is helpful to be aware of the distinctive features of some of the major variations.

Finally, the unit includes a case study of challenging camp training programs as developed and used by a major West Coast camping ministry.

James R. Crosby, James Rands, P. Richard Bunger, and Wesley E. Harty combine in this unit to place some practical program building on the foundations established in Unit 1.

4

Program Principles

James R. Crosby

- *Program Related to Objectives*
- *Program Related to Personnel*
- *Program Related to Uniqueness*
- *Program Related to Safety*
- *Program Related to Schedule*

Camp programming has been changing. In the beginning days of organized camping, leaders were prone to think of program strictly in terms of time schedules, places, and events. Today, our concept of

JAMES R. CROSBY (Th.M., Dallas Theological Seminary) is professor of Christian education, Dallas Bible College, Dallas, Texas. He has been program director at Sky Ranch, Denton, Texas, active in CCI, and teaches a camping course at Dallas Bible College.

program includes everything that occurs in the life of the camper from the time he first enters camp until the day he departs. Thus, if Charlie Camper watches with fascination as a redheaded woodpecker snatches bread crumbs from a bird feeder that Charlie made in craft class, this is program. For these events often become the valuable teaching moments in the life of the camper.

Such understanding of program provides a major challenge for camp leaders. It means the camp program must be flexible and creative to the extent that each camper is afforded the opportunity for a quality camp experience. The schedule of daily events must not be so highly structured and formalized that the camper cannot come into contact with the God of Creation because camp leaders keep him too busy.

Program, then, is defined as both the planned and unplanned content of the camper's camp experience. *Schedule* is the organization of the camper's day. A key word for both areas is flexibility.

A number of areas are to be considered in programming. These include objectives, personnel, uniqueness, safety, and scheduling.

PROGRAM RELATED TO OBJECTIVES

Programming is not an end in itself. Rather it is one of the strong links in the educational cycle. Programming is an incorporation of specific objectives enabling camp leadership to meet specific needs. A common error in camp planning is to *begin* with program. Experience and instinct still produce acceptable results. But fully effective programming knows its objectives, as illustrated in the educational wheel below.[1]

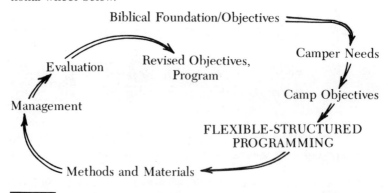

Biblical Foundation/Objectives

Evaluation

Revised Objectives, Program

Camper Needs

Management

Camp Objectives

FLEXIBLE-STRUCTURED PROGRAMMING

Methods and Materials

---

1. Adapted from Lois LeBar, *Focus on People in Church Education* (Westwood, N.J.: Revell, 1968), p. 27.

Note the expression "flexible-structured programming." At first this may seem a contradiction in terms. Actually, it is a recognition of variables that need to be balanced for fullest effectiveness. There *must* be basic structure and organization in camp. But the danger is to be overly structured. Flexibility, on the other hand, enables leadership to be alert for unexpected opportunities and the varying interests of different groups of campers.

The camp program will take into account the many interest levels found in campers: curiosity about nature, a bent for competition, love for adventure, enthusiasm for play, the compulsion to gain acceptance from peers. But the supreme objective for the Christian camp program centers in the Great Commission: to make disciples of all campers.

A Christian camp can be termed successful only to the degree that this objective is fulfilled. But what in specific terms does discipling entail in the camp setting?

Loren Fischer offers this definition of a Christian disciple:

> He (the disciple) is one who has believed Jesus Christ to be the Son of God and Saviour of men, has committed himself to Christ for salvation from sin, for control of his life and for fulfillment of purpose. He is an adherent who is sovereignly chosen and yet voluntarily binds himself in commitment to Christ and purposes to maintain a consistent loyalty to Him by abiding in the Word, by manifesting the life of Christ in daily behavior, by sharing the Gospel to the unsaved and by training any new convert in how to be available to God for renewing his own life and in converting the lost.[2]

Discipleship, then, is that quality of life in the camper that displays a Christ-centered value system. Camping provides an unusual opportunity for developing such a value system in young Christians. Of interest here is a camping definition developed in a camp course at George Williams College: "Camping is an educational experience for an individual using the unique environments of a camp to continue the developing process of the individual in the areas of social, mental, physical and spiritual, with emphasis on the spiritual, implemented for the campers through trained staff."[3]

Five features of camping can be identified that contribute to camping's effectiveness as an environment for discipling the Christian. These features suggest factors to consider when planning camp program.

TOTAL INVOLVEMENT

When a camper comes to camp, he is taken away from many influences in his home life that conflict with spiritual growth. The camper finds himself engulfed in the camp atmosphere twenty-four hours a day.

---

2. Loren Fischer, "The Task and Method of Discipling" (Lecture notes, Dallas Theological Seminary, Summer Session, 1974).
3. Students of Camping and Outdoor Education, "Values in the Field of Camping," mimeographed (George Williams College, n.d.), p. 12.

COMMUNITY LIFE

Coming from a world in which he may feel unimportant, the camper finds himself in a world designed specifically for him. A successful experience in group living at camp has obvious carry-over advantages when the camper returns home.

OUTDOOR LIVING

The coming of campers into a different and, in most cases, unfamiliar world of people and outdoor experiences tends to put all the campers on common social ground. This gives each one a chance to shed previously formed social expectations and images. Past successes are less significant and past failures less threatening.

TIME AND TIMELINESS

The flexibility of the program gives campers a chance to do things they have not had opportunity to do before and to enjoy these activities over an extended time.

SINGLE PURPOSE ADMINISTRATION

The administration's only purpose during the camping season is to devote itself completely to the camper's experience. Its effect is not weakened by spreading itself out among a number of unrelated concerns.[4]

Finally, it should be noted that while the program of a Christian camp is assumed to have a spiritual tone, care must be taken to guard that objective in actual practice.

Skits or cabin pranks that are in poor taste are sometimes introduced from non-Christian sources. Books, magazines, radios, and cassette tape players are part of the informal program that, when misused, can seriously affect the spiritual tone of the camp. Likewise, the standards of camp music need to be guarded. Camp offers a rich opportunity to increase appreciation for quality music.

PROGRAM RELATED TO PERSONNEL

Program must never be viewed apart from personnel, for at camp

---

4. Ibid., pp. 13-14.

people are an essential resource. Four persons directly involved with the program are the camp director, the program director, the counselor, and the camper.

CAMP DIRECTOR

The camp director provides the overall initiative and direction for quality programming. He must be a student of both program and people and must bring the two together. An initial step in accomplishing this is thorough research; the camp director will draw upon books, magazines, and as much personal observation as possible.

The director will find it invaluable to take notes and file ideas. He will build a catalog of program materials that fit his camp's operating philosophy.

Christian Camping International and the American Camping Association schedule regional and national conferences which provide extensive program resources, useful not only for directors but also for all staff members.

PROGRAM DIRECTOR

The program director's role is to plan and evaluate program possibilities that are consistent with the camp's spiritual objectives. A broad program field is open in camping: outdoor living, citizenship training, conservation awareness, adventure, recreation, crafts and skills, group activity. Vital social values grow through cooperative planning, small-group living, and leadership opportunities. From these many possibilities the program director develops program for campers.

COUNSELOR

The counselor is a most important link in the personnel chain, for he touches the camper most often. While the counselor need not master every program activity, he should possess a sound knowledge of the entire program in order to be able to help his campers benefit in every way. A basic premise in camping is that activities are more rewarding when elementary skills are acquired. These lay the groundwork for growth in competence.

Since campers instinctively seek models to guide them in spiritual and social development, the counselor becomes a living program resource for the camper. The quality of the person is as important to campers as the skills a counselor may possess.

CAMPER

The camper's contribution to program development may be overlooked. Careful observation and evaluation are always in order to measure the effectiveness of a program. Some camps devise a camper evaluation form to allow the camper to give his or her impressions of the camp.

Many camps create a camper council comprising representatives from each tent or cabin. The council evaluates activities in progress and makes suggestions for additional program features. The value of such a council depends on the maturity of the council members and the skill possessed by leaders in guiding discussions and interpreting camper responses.

PROGRAM RELATED TO UNIQUENESS

Program planning involves giving consideration to the uniqueness or indigenous factor. *Webster's New World Dictionary* defines *indigenous* as "born, growing, or produced naturally in a region or country; native."

In respect to program, indigenous means the camp should include activities and events peculiar to its region. The indigenous principle encourages efforts to capitalize on unique topographical, geological, and climatic features. Thus a camp on the coast might feature surfing, a camp in the West could sponsor a rodeo, and a camp in the north woods might emphasize canoeing.

An example of a camp alert to its local opportunities is Camp Peniel, located in the heart of the Hill Country of central Texas. Peniel has on its property one of the oldest buildings in that section of the country. The building's colorful history gave the camp director the idea of using drama to share with campers the story of the building and the early Indian raids. The camp staff applied dramatics and grease paint to spotlight a truly indigenous feature of this camp.

Each camp has indigenous program possibilities. God has blessed His creation with interesting features that, with creative imagination, can be woven into the fabric of the camp program. The psalmist wrote (Pslam 104: 1-4,24):

Bless the LORD, O my soul!
O LORD my God, Thou art very
    great;
Thou art clothed with splendor
    and majesty,
Covering Thyself with light as
    with a cloak,
Stretching out heaven like a
    tent curtain.
He lays the beams of His upper
    chambers in the waters;
He makes the clouds His
    chariot;
He walks upon the wings of
    the wind;
He makes the winds His mes-
    sengers,
Flaming fire His ministers.
. . . .
O LORD, how many are Thy
    works!
In wisdom Thou hast made
    them all;
The earth is full of Thy pos-
    sessions.

Program Related to Safety

While evangelism and discipleship maintain their rightful place in evangelical camps, an important perspective on program is safety for camper and staff. Accordingly, when priorities among camp objectives are established, health and safety procedures must be ranked among the first. L. Ted Johnson and Lee M. Kingsley sound this word of warning: "There is real danger that an ambitious safety program could reduce activities and restrict campers. Camping must be fun and adventure. A certain element of the unknown must be in all of the activities. Camping must also be safe and keep campers from exposure which will produce unnecessary accidents or stress."[5]

Suggestions for adequate safety standards include the following:

1. Adopt the high standards of the American Camping Association and Christian Camping International. ACA's section on health and safety in *Standards for Organized Camps* provides an excellent guide,[6] and CCI's *Foundations for Excellence* has a similar emphasis.[7]
2. Have available competent professional medical staff. *Standards for Organized Camps* asks: "Does the *Family* or *Resident* camp have in residence on its staff a licensed physician and/or registered nurse accredited to practice in the state in which the camp is located? Are all staff members given fundamental knowledge of procedure to follow in the event of health emergencies?"[8]
3. Inform, educate, and train the camp staff. In addition to observing ACA and CCI standards, every camp must deal with its particular safety hazards. These might be poison oak or ivy, stinging nettle, ticks, or mosquitoes. Even the weather can be a source of danger: severe thunderstorms, tornadoes, fires, floods. Safety procedures must be planned.
4. Enforce the camp's safety rules. Train the staff in safety and educate campers to dangers. The best safety device yet developed is a conscientious, trained staff person fulfilling his responsibility for camper safety.

---

5. L. Ted Johnson and Lee M Kingsley, *Blueprint for Quality* (Chicago: Harvest, 1969), p. 155.
6. American Camping Association, *Standards for Organized Camps* (Martinsville, Ind.: ACA, n.d.), p. 15.
7. Christian Camping International, *Foundations for Excellence* (Somonauk, Ill.: CCI, 1977).
8. ACA, *Standards for Organized Camps*, p. 15.

PROGRAM RELATED TO SCHEDULE

The organization of the program—the way the various parts are arranged in the daily schedule—is an important factor in camp operation. Thus, the movement from one type of activity to another type needs careful consideration. Going from a highly exciting recreational activity to a devotional time, for example, requires opportunity for adjustment.

How much time is allowed for the activities and where they are placed in the schedule are likewise key considerations in effective programming. The following are other factors to keep in mind:

CAMPER FOCUS

"Camp is for the camper!" We repeat it often, but the import of the concept can be forgotten in our scheduling. The camper can be lost in the hurry of maintaining the daily program.

A camp can encourage camper focus when there is a scheduling emphasis on small group relationships and flexible program structure.

CONTINUITY

An undergirding principle is to maintain continuity from season to season without getting into a rut. A camp will find it valuable to develop well-proved camp traditions. But a camp needs change too. Every camp will benefit from fresh scheduling ideas to keep things from becoming dull and commonplace to the campers. Schedule continuity for security and schedule innovation for freshness will help provide quality programming.

BALANCE

A third perspective on scheduling is balance. The challenge is to provide recreation, Bible teaching, group activity, and individual time in a productive relationship.

Schedule balance is influenced by such factors as the length of the camp session. Thus, a two-week session provides more room for activity variety than an overnight retreat. Likewise, the schedule is affected by the need for both active and quiet programming. In planning, such factors require careful scrutiny.

Climate also should not be overlooked in developing schedule balance. In some areas hot weather may dictate placing the more demanding activities in the cooler morning hours, which allows for a slower pace under the afternoon sun.

Concerning the need for balance, the CCI program pamphlet, *Foundations for Excellence*, states, "A proper balance will be developed between emphases such as competitiveness, achievement, team and individual activities, external awards, rules, adult pressure and control."[9]

FLEXIBILITY

Flexibility and adaptability are two critical qualities that need careful consideration as leaders block out the camp schedule. One technique for attaining flexibility is "backward planning."

Backward planning, as the title suggests, involves thinking and working back to front when scheduling. Start with the last activity of the day and schedule events from that point to the first activity of the day. The advantage of this approach is that the program director can plan time between activities in a more realistic fashion. Backward planning also alerts leaders to the sleep needs of campers according to the various age levels. The following illustration diagrams the method of "backward planning."

SCHEDULE

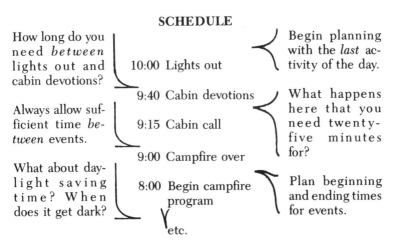

How long do you need *between* lights out and cabin devotions?

Always allow sufficient time *between* events.

What about daylight saving time? When does it get dark?

10:00 Lights out

9:40 Cabin devotions

9:15 Cabin call

9:00 Campfire over

8:00 Begin campfire program

etc.

Begin planning with the *last* activity of the day.

What happens here that you need twenty-five minutes for?

Plan beginning and ending times for events.

While there is a great variety of possible daily schedules, depending on type of camp, camping approach, and program philosophy,

9. Christian Camping International, *Foundations for Excellence* (Somonauk, Ill.: CCI, 1977), p. 2.

there are some basic schedule outlines. A representative one is suggested by Joy Mackay:

7:00 Reveille	1:45 Trading Post
7:30 Flag raising	2:00 Rest hour
7:40 Quiet time	3:15 Third activity
8:00 Breakfast	4:30 Free swim
8:30 Cabin and camp cleanup	5:45 Supper
9:00 Bible study	6:45 Evening program
10:15 First activity	9:15 Cabin call
11:30 Second activity	9:40 Cabin devotions
1:00 Dinner	10:00 Taps[10]

Mackay's recommendation for Sunday scheduling is also helpful: "Sunday should be a special day for your campers, a more relaxed time. It may be some campers' introduction to the real significance of the Lord's Day. Make it both a spiritually profitable and an enjoyable day, with a change of pace and a different or modified daily schedule."[11]

10. Joy Mackay, *Creative Counseling for Christian Camps* (Wheaton, Ill.: Scripture Press, 1966), p. 70.
11. Ibid., p. 71.

SUGGESTIONS FOR STUDY

1. Illustrate the difference between program and schedule.
2. In what specific ways can counselors help campers evaluate the camp program?
3. The chapter lists four different personnel and their relationship to the program. In addition to these, what other personnel have a share in the program, and what is that part?
4. In what ways can the camp's program be genuinely camper centered? Be specific.
5. In what specific ways should the program contribute to the development of a Christ-centered value system?
6. Write out a statement of philosophy of program, attempting to include implications related to the camp's total operating philosophy.
7. Develop some indigenous program ideas for a camp with which you are acquainted.
8. Using the "backward planning" technique, plan a typical day's schedule for junior-age campers.
9. Evaluate a camp program from a Luke 2:52 point of reference by listing in what areas the camp activities contribute to developing a balanced Christian life.
10. Evaluate a specific camp's schedule in the light of the four perspectives on scheduling discussed in the chapter. What are the areas of strength? What areas need improvement?

RESOURCES

Dimock, Hendley S., ed. *Administration of the Modern Camp*. New York: Association, 1948.

Hammett, Catherine T., and Musselman, Virginia. *The Camp Program Book*. New York: Association, 1951.

Johnson, L. Ted, and Kingsley, Lee M. *Blueprint for Quality*. Chicago: Harvest, 1969.

Mackay, Joy. *Creative Counseling for Christian Camps*. Wheaton, Ill.: Scripture Press, 1966.

Mitchell, A. Viola; Crawford, Ida B.; and Robberson, Julia D. *Camp Counseling*. 4th ed. Philadelphia: Saunders, 1970.

Reimann, Lewis C. *The Successful Camp*. Ann Arbor: U. of Michigan, 1958.

Todd, Floyd, and Todd, Pauline. *Camping for Christian Youth*. New York: Harper & Row, 1963.

Webb, Kenneth B. *Light from a Thousand Campfires*. Minneapolis: Burgess, 1960.

5

Program Activities

James R. Crosby

- *Spiritual Growth Activities*
- *Physical Skill Activities*
- *Social Relationship Activities*
- *Recreational Activities*

Concerning Jesus, Luke wrote, "[He] kept increasing in wisdom and stature, and in favor with God and men" (Luke 2:52).

This verse identifies an ultimate goal of evangelical camping: the development of the whole person committed to God. The task of this chapter is to show how the camp program can minister to that whole person. The chapter will suggest four principal areas of program for evangelical camping: spiritual growth, physical skills, social relationships, and recreational activities.

SPIRITUAL GROWTH ACTIVITIES

Spiritual growth activities in camp include the areas of evangelism, Bible study, and worship.

While basic spiritual content will not differ markedly from content used in other places, the camp setting provides unique points of contact. Thus, the counselor training program should instruct in how to use the animals, birds, plant life, and natural terrain of camp as a bridge in spiritual discussions with campers. For example, as the roots of the trees at camp dig deep into the soil for nourishment, so we must dig into and study God's Word to find our nourishment.

Counselors should be encouraged to study the Scriptures for examples of illustrations from nature as well as to do research on nature itself.

BIBLE STUDY

The camp environment provides an abundance of natural resources for Bible study. A basic principle is to support a carefully planned curriculum by using the immediate camp surroundings to the fullest.

The inductive approach is a favorite method for Bible studies in camp. This method requires effort and patience, since the camper himself is directly involved in the learning process.

Inductive Bible study includes three basic steps:

1. Observation—focusing on the reading and rereading of the passage being studied. In a prayerful and imaginative process, the student notes the words, structure, literary form, and atmosphere of the passage.
2. Interpretation—seeking to understand the meaning of the text. This can be developed through use of the standard journalistic questions: Who?, What?, Where?, When?, Why?, and How?
3. Application—determining what the interpretation means to the camper's life. He is then encouraged to appropriate the truths.

A suggested listing of outdoor-oriented Scriptures that can be used in an inductive-study approach are included at the end of the chapter.

WORSHIP

Fundamentally, worship is the personal response of a believer as he witnesses something of God's nature or character. It may relate to praise, adoration, thanksgiving, prayer, reverence, trust, hope, or respect. Worship is often aided by some vehicle of expression such as music, audible prayer, testimonies, Bible reading, or devotional teaching.

The task of camp leadership is to provide opportunities for genuine worship. Camps are not restricted to the chapel or to the usual worship forms. Camping offers the opportunity of a new setting.

In addition, camp has the advantage of fewer distractions. An uncluttered environment and unhurried schedule can furnish a welcome change from the helter-skelter pace at home. Moreover, camping provides trained leadership who reflect Christ-centered living. As the camper is guided in the wonders of worship, the power of example can hardly be exaggerated. And, perhaps for the first time, a camper may discover that he or she can worship someplace other than in church.

Most significant of all, camping places the camper close to God's creation. The psalmist exclaimed: "When I consider Thy heavens, the work of Thy fingers, the moon and the stars, which Thou hast ordained; what is man, that Thou dost take thought of him? And the son of man, that Thou dost care for him?" (Psalm 8:3-4).

Finally, worship can be expressed in a variety of times and places. Consider some of these opportunities:

1. Spontaneous fellowship—Campers led by the Spirit may share verses, thoughts, prayers, or songs. Such times generate freedom of participation.
2. Table worship—During the meal the camp leadership cultivates the atmosphere for table worship. After the meal the campers share in a short devotional, a Bible passage, or brief reading from a devotional guide.
3. Cabin worship—Camps usually plan a time of cabin devotions, often when the campers are settled and ready for bed.
4. Study groups—Worship in study groups is especially meaningful for teenagers. A variety of approaches may be used: sentence prayer, antiphonal reading, praise and thanksgiving thoughts.
5. Early morning worship—In this approach, the schedule allows for a morning worship time. If the event is optional, care must

be exercised that early risers do not disturb those who choose another worship time.

6. Moonlight worship—A cabin group may worship on a night hike or as part of a camp-out.

7. Musical expression—This is one of the great avenues of worship available. Camps should provide both structured and spontaneous opportunities for such expression. Worship values are found in the great hymns of the faith as well as in contemporary gospel music. There has been a resurgence of singing the Scriptures, especially the Psalms, which is a helpful means of worship.

8. Dramatics—Well-done choral readings, Bible plays, and devotional monologues provide opportunities for worship experiences.

9. Campfire programs—The campfire setting encourages creative worship times. When fun-type songs are used first, careful transition should lead campers into devotional songs.

10. Lakefront services—These have been used by many camps as the setting for a Sunday morning service emphasizing Jesus' experiences at the Sea of Galilee.

11. Worship at flag-lowering—This is choice time for reflection about the Creator, as well as for thoughts on patriotism and Christian citizenship. Choral reading of a Psalm by a cabin group can enhance the service of worship.

> Praise the LORD!
> Praise God in His sanctuary;
> Praise Him in His mighty ex-
>   panse.
> Praise Him for His mighty
>   deeds;
> Praise Him according to His ex-
>   cellent greatness.
> Psalm 150:1-2

PHYSICAL SKILL ACTIVITIES

Christian camping concerns itself with the spiritual integration of the whole person. This touches all areas of living. Thus, the Christian life may be as well expressed through how a person plays a game or responds to a natural phenomenon as through a formal religious exercise.

Some camp physical activities may have specific biblical application. Horsemanship, for example, might be related to several passages (James 3:3; Job 39:19-25). Such references can well be included in general background for the activity, although the value of a skill does not lie in a particular Bible reference. Physical development and skill acquisition contribute to the wholeness of the person, and this has spiritual implications.

A significant value of the physical skills also lies in the modeling of the Christian life by capable and respected instructors. Spiritual truth may be gained through the warm association of a camper with a godly woodcraft instructor as well as from a Bible class.

The list of physical activities that might be included in the camp program is extensive, and each has value when kept in camp-purpose perspective. A general guideline for planning is that camp has special value when the program majors in activities not commonly found at home.

Physical skill activities may be discussed in six major classifications, though the lines between them are frequently crossed. Proper equipment, appropriate field markings, and correct playing procedures should accompany instruction in these activities. Qualified instructors are, of course, required.

The relationship between program and the camp setting becomes evident when physical skill activities are discussed. Woodcraft skills can be practiced on an asphalt parking lot but with minimal rewards for the campers. Since an abundance of resource materials is readily available for the activities mentioned below, we will be content simply to discuss the categories and point out some of the values and cautions related to them.

SPORTS

Sports activity includes all team sports and the more familiar outdoor games. Ball games are common fare on camp programs. Yet to major in these games played back home is to deprive the camper of many experiences he can find only at camp. Creative camp leaders will make camp an opportunity to enjoy new activities.

Camp leaders differ as to the value of strong competition between cabin groups or between teams established for the camp period. Some leaders, taking advantage of the enthusiasm and motivation for participation that campers find in competing, build week-long programs around competition. Others feel it is better to mingle campers each day by creating new groups each time a team sport is scheduled. The difficulty of achieving team balance causes some camps to play down extensive competition.

WATERFRONT ACTIVITY

Swimming , diving, and boating in their various forms are recognized as popular camp program features. When water skills are taught, the program value of the beach or pool is enhanced.

In spite of a good safety record, camp waterfront activities are still the most potentially dangerous part of the camp program. There is no excuse for any compromise on waterfront safety, and certified, conscientious personnel must be on duty at all activity times.

Swimming is, of course, the waterfront activity that normally serves the greatest number of campers. This is a traditional part of camp life, although canoeing, sailing, and water skiing have grown rapidly in popularity at Christian camps. When equipment and competent leadership are available, some camps have offered instruction in scuba diving for older campers. However, scuba diving, like water skiing, serves a limited number of campers each activity period.

GAMES

The distinction between games and sports is rather arbitrary. Usually a game involves smaller teams, perhaps two on each side, and is played on a small court.

Such games as box hockey, shuffleboard, tetherball, and horseshoes offer pleasant outdoor activity times for campers. Rainy days will draw campers to indoor games such as checkers and chess. Table tennis is a game for all days, indoors or out.

Group games not associated with a ball or court, such as capture the flag or counselor hunt, are also popular at camp. Bible games and quiz contests can be valuable teaching devices, especially if they are not overused.

NATURE STUDY AND WOODCRAFT

Teaching about the flora and fauna native to the camp area requires special preparation. However, wherever there are twigs, cones, shells, stones, grasses, seed pods, or mosses, both nature and craft instructors can keep busy. Nature crafts are inexpensive and instructive, and most campsites offer considerable resources for them.

Some wildlife, often more than either campers or staff realize, will be found in every camp. A feeding area will help reveal their presence. An early morning bird hike can add new trophies to the camp's collection of identified birds, whose pictures adorn the dining hall bird board.

How many trees and shrubs grow on your camp? (One camp leader identified one hundred fifty different species of grasses, trees, shrubs, vines, weeds, and flowering plants that grew on a thirty-five-acre camp.)

Not every camper will become deeply involved in nature study, but many will, especially with enthusiastic guidance.

Woodcraft skills can be practiced at an outpost camp on or near the main camp property. Tent pitching, fire building, outdoor cooking, star identification, compass use, and weather prediction are some of the activities here. Skills learned in the outpost camp prepare campers for camping adventures to come.

CRAFTS

Worthy campcraft will demand some creativity. Plastic punch-out and-glue projects have short life and minimal value.

Wood and leather work, braiding and macrame, sand casting, weaving, painting, and sculpting—the list of possible crafts is limited only by the leader's imagination.

Campers with less aptitude or enthusiasm for sports and games will often respond to crafts. Again, when the instructor is a warm Christian, there is opportunity for spiritual growth.

As with sports and games, the camp should major in crafts the camper is not likely to find in the home community.[1]

---

1. See chapter 6, "Arts and Crafts," for a full discussion of crafts.

HIGH ADVENTURE

Many camps are adding high adventure programs away from the home base to minister to the older camper who may have spent several seasons in the resident program. Possible activities include rock climbing and rappelling, white water canoeing and kayaking, and orienteering.

All the above physical activities possess value for the camper as they become part of his storehouse of knowledge and experience and contribute to the wholeness of personal development. The spiritual worth of adventure under the guidance of Christian leaders is a large camping program plus.[2]

SOCIAL RELATIONSHIP ACTIVITIES

MUSIC

How empty life would be without music! Camp authorities agree:

It is the most natural thing in the world for happy campers to sing whenever and wherever they are; conversely, campers who sing can scarcely avoid being happy. Song should burst forth as spontaneously as mushrooms after a rain, for the miles fly by while hiking, dishes seem to almost dry themselves and even mediocre paddlers swing into a space-covering rhythm when there is a song in the air. Good music is a great leavening agent; few fail to succumb to a catchy tune, a strong rhythm or the sheer beauty of a lovely melody. No camper or counselor should return home without a complete repertoire of good, new (to him) songs in his head as well as fond memories of frequently sung old favorites.[3]

Sing often. Many camps join in a chorus or two after meals. Select songs that fit the week's theme or program emphasis. Songs should be of high quality, make you feel glad to sing, and leave a sense of satisfaction. Who has not experienced the staying power of a catchy singing commercial? Camp music, be it good, bad, or indifferent, has that same adhesive quality.

You can do without accompaniment if necessary, although a piano is great for dining hall singing. Guitars make fine accompaniment. Why not try a harmonica too?

Songleaders need not be professionals, but they should have a sense of tone and rhythm and the ability to make people want to sing.

In teaching songs, use audio-visuals such as the overhead pro-

---

2. See chapter 7, "Specialized Programs," a discussion of mobile camping.
3. Viola Mitchell, Julia D. Robberson, and June W. Obley, *Camp Counseling*, 5th ed. (Philadelphia: Saunders, 1977), pp. 221-222.

jector, flip charts, butcher paper tacked to the wall, and similar aids. "Let the word of Christ richly dwell within you, with all wisdom teaching and admonishing one another with psalms and hymns and spiritual songs, singing with thankfulness in your hearts to God" (Col. 3:16). "Speaking to one another in psalms and hymns and spiritual songs, singing and making melody with your heart to the Lord" (Eph. 5:19).

SKITS

In the pressured society we live in today, skits and humor can play a significant role. Their judicious use has a beneficial place in camp programs.

Humor can tear down barriers and prejudices, relieve tension, and provide bridges between counselors and campers. "A merry heart maketh a cheerful countenance, but by sorrow of the heart the spirit is broken" (Prov. 15:13, KJV).

RECREATIONAL ACTIVITIES

Webster's Third New International Dictionary defines *recreation* as "refreshment of the strength and spirits after toil: diversion, play." The word itself communicates the idea of recreating. Christian recreation should refresh the whole man.

Recreation provides healthy fun, releases pent-up feelings, helps a person know himself better, helps him know others, develops imagination, creates a sense of belonging, improves physical and mental skills, and helps fulfill emotional needs.

The following are basic categories of recreational type activities:

INSTRUCTIONAL ACTIVITIES

Many camps engage specialists for these activities where regular instruction is provided. Typical activities include riflery, archery, lifesaving, campcraft, horsemanship, and arts and crafts.

RAINY DAY ACTIVITIES

Some activities will be adapted to inclement weather.

EVENING PROGRAM SPECIALS

Special activities provide a change of pace from the normal

schedule and fit the "extravaganza" category. Examples would include stunt night and music festival.

SPECIAL DAY PROGRAMS

Special day programs are activities which have been designed around a special theme. This would include track and field events, backwards days, and aquatic carnivals. Often these arise from the regular program activities and may be a culmination of them. Or they may be developed from special interests of the campers.

GROUP LIVING ACTIVITIES

A group living activity occurs within the cabin group and stems from the group's interests.

CONSERVATION PROJECTS

Conservation projects are those activities that contribute to the camper's understanding of ecology and help to perserve the camp's natural resources.

MISSION ACTIVITIES

Mission education may be provided through a visiting missionary or a film; or an outreach project may be carried out in a community near the camp.[4]

---

4. Adapted from card file by H. Jean Berger, *Program Activities for Camps*, 2d ed., (Minneapolis: Burgess, 1964).

SUGGESTIONS FOR STUDY

1. What other camp program activities are you familiar with that were not discussed in this chapter? What place could these have in the overall objective of making disciples?
2. What criteria must camp leaders keep in mind as they plan program activities?
3. How would you justify the inclusion of recreational activities in a Christian camp?
4. What is the most significant camp program activity that you have personally participated in? Explain your choice.
5. What relation should there be between camp program and the cultural life-style patterns of the campers?
6. In respect to discipleship, analyze the program of a camp with which you are familiar. Give suggestions as to how an emphasis on making disciples could be strengthened.
7. Make a list of your five favorite recreational games or activities. Be prepared to explain and demonstrate one of these to the rest of the class.
8. Draw up a chart of activities under the four principal program categories of this chapter.

RESOURCES

OUTDOOR-ORIENTED SCRIPTURE REFERENCES FOR BIBLE STUDY

THE NATURAL RESOURCES GOD HAS PROVIDED IN OUR WORLD

Gen. 1-2—The Creation story
Psalm 8—Man's place in God's world
Psalm 19:1-6—The heavenly message
Psalm 24:1-2—The earth is the Lord's
Psalm 65:9-13—The blessing of rain
Psalms 92, 93, 95, 96, 97, 98, 100, and 148—Psalms of praise for the world
Psalm 104—God's Word on ecology

MAN'S DEPENDENCE UPON GOD FOR HIS BASIC NEEDS

Gen. 1:26-31—Interdependence of plants, animals, and man. A basic ecological passage.
Gen. 8:22—Dependability
Psalm 23—The Shepherd Psalm
Psalm 36:5-10—The steadfastness of God's love
Psalm 65:9-13—Abundance of the harvest
Psalm 104—The plan of the world
Psalm 111:5—God's provision of food
Psalm 147:7-9, 14-18—God's gifts
Prov. 6:6-11—Lessons from the ant
Song of Sol. 2:11—The end of winter and the beginning of spring
Isa. 40:28—God is not weary
Isa. 41:18-20—God's provision of rivers and trees
Isa. 44:14-16—Gift of fire
Isa. 55—Rain cycle
Matt. 6:25-33—God's care
Mark 4:26-29—Seedtime and harvest

CAMPING EXPERIENCE IN OLD TESTAMENT

Abraham—Gen. 12:1-9; 13:14-18; 15:5-6
Jacob—Gen. 28:10-17
Moses—Wilderness; also Exod. 3:1-7; 15:22-27; 19:17-20
Elijah—1 Kings 17—19
Ezra—Ezra 8:15-20
Amos—Amos 7:14-15

JESUS THE OUTDOORS MAN

Matt. 5:1-20; Luke 5:1-12—Teaching

Luke 4:1-13; 6:12—Times for prayer

Matt. 6:25-33; 10:29-31; 13:31-32; 16:3-4; Luke 12:22-31, 54-55; 15:3-7—Reference to plants, animals, birds, sky

ELEMENTS OF NATURE

Stones—Deut. 8:7-9; 32:4; Job 28:1-2, 5-6; Psalm 18:2; 62:7

Seeds—Matt. 13:31-32

Stars—Gen. 1:14-18

Moon—Psalm 148:1,9,13,14

The Weather—Gen. 9:12-17; Job 37:16; 38:37; Psalm 135:7; 147:7-8,16,18

PROGRAM MATERIALS

GENERAL

Berger, H. Jean. *Program Activities for Camps*, 2d ed. Minneapolis: Burgess, 1964. Basic resource tool for program leaders.

Hammett, Catherine T., and Musselman, Virginia. *The Camp Program Book*. New York: Association, 1951. Outstanding secular title encompassing virtually every camp activity.

Mackay, Joy. *Creative Camping*, Wheaton, Ill.: Victor, 1977. Practical handbook with solid emphasis on campcraft skills.

Mitchell, A. Viola; Crawford, Ida B; and Robberson, Julia D. *Camp Counseling*, 4th ed. Philadelphia: Saunders, 1970. An encyclopedic resource tool with just as much on program as on counseling.

Riviere, Bill. *The Family Camper's Bible*. Garden City, N.Y.: Doubleday, 1975. Though geared for the family, Riviere's work is of great value to youth camping. The author strikes a happy medium between luxury and primitive camping. Many suggestions to make campcraft activities both educational and fun.

Todd, Floyd, and Todd, Pauline. *Camping for Christian Youth*. New York: Harper & Row, 1963. Synthesized approach to organized evangelical camping with thumbnail sketch of camp activities.

SPIRITUAL GROWTH ACTIVITIES

Evangelism and discipleship.

Coleman, Robert E. *The Master Plan of Evangelism*. Westwood, N.J.: Revell, 1963. Follows Christ's methods with His disciples. A book for careful study and restudy.

Getz, Gene A. *The Measure of a Man*. Glendale, Calif.: Regal, 1974. Built around a study of 1 Timothy 3 and Titus 1 with exercise sections at the end of each chapter. Excellent for staff Bible studies.

Hendricks, Howard G. *Say it with Love*. Wheaton, Ill.: Victor, 1972. Good for leadership challenge. Leader's guide would be most useful in counselor training.

Henrichsen, Walter A. *Disciples Are Made–Not Born*. Wheaton, Ill.: Victor, 1974. Gives useful insights into discipling. Avoids the "canned" approach.

Bible study.

Jensen, Irving L. *Independent Bible Study*. Chicago: Moody, 1963. Especially strong in analytical and chart-making techniques.

PHYSICAL SKILLS ACTIVITIES

Horsemanship.

Anderson, C. W. *Heads-Up Heels Down*. New York: Macmillan, 1961.

Holmelund, Paul. *The Art of Horsemanship*. New York: Barnes & Noble, 1962.

Taylor, Louis. *Ride American*. New York: Harper & Row, 1963.

Archery.

Burke, Edmond H. *Archery Handbook*. New York: Arco, 1954. History and development of archery plus make-it-yourself information. Illustrated.

Forbes, Thomas A. *New Guide to Better Archery*. Harrisburg, Pa.: Stackpole, 1960. Very comprehensive, including bowhunting. Illustrated.

Whiffen, Larry C. *Shooting the Bow*. Milwaukee: Bruce, 1966. Designed for the beginner. Illustrated.

Outpost camping.

Boy Scouts of America. *Boy Scout Handbook*. New Brunswick, N.J.: BSA, 1966.

Colby, C. B., and Angier, Bradford. *The Art and Science of Taking to the Woods*. New York: Collier, 1970. Thorough investigation of equipment, skills, and techniques for enjoying nature lore.

Glass, Walter. *Key to Knots and Splices*. New York: Key, 1959. Describes and illustrates hundreds of knots, ties, lashes, and splices.

Hammett, Catherine. *Your Own Book of Campcraft*. New York: Pocket, 1950. Basic pioneering skills such as fire building, outdoor cookery, and knotcraft.

Lynn, Gordon. *Camping and Camp Crafts*. New York: Golden, 1959.

Riviere, Bill. *Backcountry Camping*. Garden City, N.Y.: Doubleday, 1971. Practical advice on nearly every aspect of wilderness camping. Written by one of America's finest outdoor authorities.
Whelen, Townsend, and Angier, Bradford. *On Your Own in the Wilderness*. New York: Galahad, 1958. Solid outdoor wisdom from two veterans of trail and wilderness camping.
Nature crafts.
Bale, R. O. *Creative Nature Crafts*. Minneapolis: Burgess, 1959.
Tangerman, E. J. *Whittling and Woodcarving*. New York: Dover, 1936. Don't let the publication date disappoint you; this title offers valuable pointers for beginning a wood lore emphasis in your camp's craft program.
van der Smissen, Betty, and Goering, Oswald H. *Nature-Oriented Activities*. 2d ed. Ames, Iowa: Iowa State U., 1968.
Zim, Herbert S., and Martin, Alexander. *Trees*. New York: Golden, 1952. Put this one in your hip pocket for help in tree variety study and identification.
Waterfront activities.
All Red Cross and YMCA materials highly recommended.
Rohndoff, Richard H. *Camp Waterfront Programs and Management*. New York: Association, n.d.
Riviere, Bill. *Pole, Paddle and Portage*. New York: Van Nostrand-Reinhold, 1969. All about canoeing, from open-water to running the rapids. Excellent bibliography. Illustrated.

SOCIAL SKILLS ACTIVITIES

Music.

Title	Publisher/Address
Sing 'n Celebrate	WORD, Box 1790, Waco, TX 76703
Jesus Songs	BROADMAN PRESS, Nashville, TN 37234
Songbook for Saints and Sinners	AGAPE, 5707 W. Corcoran Place, Chicago, IL 60644
Songs	YOUNG LIFE, Box 1519, Colorado Springs, CO 80901
Mission 70	BROADMAN PRESS, Nashville, TN 37234
Songs for Now	
He's Everything to Me	LEXICON MUSIC, INC., c/o Sacred Songs, Waco, TX 76703
A Time to Sing	HOPE PUBLISHING CO., 5707 W. Lake St., Chicago, IL 60644
My Soapbox	NOW SOUNDS, 1415 Lake Dr., S.E., Grand Rapids, MI 49506
"NOW"	HOPE PUBLISHING CO., 5707 W. Lake St., Chicago, IL 60644

Burl Ives Song Book	BALLANTINE BOOKS, 101 Fifth Ave. New York, NY 10003
"Anywhere" Songs	INTER-VARSITY CHRISTIAN FELLOWHIP, 5206 Main St., Downers Grove, IL 60515
Songs for Fun and Fellowhip #1, 2, & 3	BROADMAN PRESS, Nashville, TN 37234
Hymnal for Young Christians	F.E.L. CHURCH PBULICATONS, LTD. 1543 W. Olympic Blvd., Los Angeles, CA 90015
A New Now Youth Folk Hymnal	HOPE PUBLISHING CO., 5707 W. Lake St., Chicago, IL 60644
Folk Hymnal for the Now Generation	SINGSPIRATION, INC., 1415 Lake Dr., S.E., Grand Rapids, MI 49506
Songs for Fun and Fellowship Abingdon Song Kit	ABINGDON PRESS, Nashville, TN 37203

(List compiled by William Haas, professor of music at Dallas Bible College, Dallas, Tex.)

Skits and stunts.
Strandberg, Arlene B., and Troup, Dick, eds. *Skits, Plays and Projects for Youth Ministries.* Tempe, Ariz.: Success With Youth, 1975. Covers the gamut of ideas for youth-centered theatrics. Highly recommended.

RECREATIONAL ACTIVITIES

Anderson, John E. *Fun with Games.* Madison, Wisc.: Dembar Education Research Serv., 1968. Gives rules and procedures for common sports and other games.

Mulac, Margaret E. *Games and Stunts.* New York: Harper & Row, 1964. Excellent games, suggestions for the school, camp, or playground.

6

Arts and Crafts

James Rands

- *The Values of Arts and Crafts*
- *The Goals of the Arts and Crafts Program*
- *The Use of Arts in Camp*
- *Types of Crafts in the Camp Setting*
- *Points to Consider in an Arts and Crafts Program*
- *Basic Listings of Craft Projects*
- *Materials Available for Camp Arts and Crafts*

JAMES RANDS (M.S., George Williams College) is minister of education, Minnetonka Community Church, Minnetonka, Minnesota. Mr. Rands has been director of Camp Moyoca (Illinois) and the teacher of camping courses at St. Paul Bible College.

The uniqueness of camping provides the evangelical church with an especially effective means of reaching and educating children and youth. A camp arts and crafts program can have a vital place in this outreach and development.

The Values of Arts and Crafts

Arts and crafts are more than a means for filling up time in a camp program. Their values are very real. Here are some of the most basic.

SUCCESS AND PERSONAL ACHIEVEMENT

Campers (as well as counselors and camp directors) are looking for opportunities to achieve personal success. The successful participation in and completion of an arts and crafts project provides one such achievement opportunity. Further, the sense of accomplishment helps form in the campers positive attitudes toward many areas including personal abilities.

SELF-WORTH

Closely related to the opportunity for success and achievement is the building of self-worth as the camper creates, participates in, and completes an arts and crafts project. He can learn that he is a competent individual. This aids in a healthy view of self and is a practical reminder of God's provision of abilities and skills.

USE OF HANDS

The manipulation of objects and tools and the stimulation of the tactual senses are often deeply satisfying. There is also some indication from Scripture that working with the hands is therapeutic in changing behavior patterns (Eph. 4:28). Encouraging a camper to work on projects that involve the hands and various senses will certainly give him a deeper awareness of his physical environment.

RELEASE OF PHYSICAL AND EMOTIONAL ENERGY

The release of physical energy results from the use of large muscles and small muscle groups. Emotional energy is often expended by hammering, banging of tools, the accompanying noise of the work, and social interaction, as well as by the shouting that often goes along with the arts and crafts program. This dissipation of physical and emotional energy provides a legitimate outlet for the camper.

CARRY-OVER

Often the skills learned in the camp setting are carried over into the "back home" life of the camper. Interests and hobbies are encouraged by exposure to and success in various arts and crafts projects. The success, the realization of personal competence, and the satisfaction gained at camp would encourage the camper to continue in these activities when he returns home.

THE GOALS OF THE ARTS AND CRAFTS PROGRAM

There are primarily two approaches to arts and crafts, both legitimate. Some campers respond more readily to one than to the other, but campers should be exposed to both.

PROCESS ORIENTATION

Process is concerned with the *involvement* in the project. The creativity, the manipulation of objects, the opportunity for expression of feelings while doing the project are all parts of process. Many of the values of arts and crafts are realized in the doing process. The younger child often responds to this aspect of arts and crafts if exposed to the concept early.

GOAL ORIENTATION

Goal is the *achieving* of an end product. There is a deep satisfaction in the completion of an undertaking. The completion and showing of a project may be an effective status symbol. The project may demonstrate a skill; it may be used as a gift. The older child may be more interested in the finished product than he is in working, but should enjoy the process of how he gets to the end product as well.

All ages of camper, including adults, are involved in experimentation. The initial satisfaction from arts and crafts comes from the process, the doing of the project. The end product is the added bonus.

The Use of Arts in Camp

The arts in camping must be geared to (1) the skills that campers bring to camp or (2) the development of skills used in the arts. As an end product, art often is of greatest interest to the older child. Involving the younger camper in the arts is a preparatory program, and a high skill level should not be expected. However, it is good to exhibit his art project at camp. There are a wide variety of usable art areas.

MUSIC

Camp music should provide for a variety of expression. The first would be group singing. For children, include the songs that children enjoy singing—fun songs, nonsense songs, ballads, and folk singing. Care should be taken that there is clear distinction between fun and nonsense songs and Christian choruses. An appreciation for good music might be developed by a well-planned camp music ministry. Often churches are introduced to fine new songs because children who have been to camp bring these songs back with them.

Campers should be encouraged to develop their abilities. There can be opportunity for solos, duets, quartets, as well as a camp choir or chorus. Some camps use music as a focal point. At the end of camp, concerts are given for the community and the families and friends of the campers.

Instrumental music is another area. Campers can be encouraged by the camp publicity to bring instruments. Provide band and orchestra practice. Group playing may be difficult but can be encouraged. The instruments that are most often brought to camp and create the most interest are those that can be used to accompany group singing. These include guitar, harmonica, and accordion.

DRAMA

The use of drama can add tremendously to the overall ministry of the camp. Dramatics may be limited to group skits or a talent night. More extensive productions can be performed for the camp community or local area. Biblical drama can be used in camp as an effective means of understanding Scripture, for dramatization of Bible stories, and as response to biblical teachings. Such use increases the interest of the camper and aids in his grasp of the Scriptures.

Dramatic projects in camp might include puppetry. The shy camper is often more inclined to participate in puppet dramatization than in other public programs. Even the quieter child will speak out and "act" in a puppet program. The making of puppets and props falls into the crafts area of camp and adds to that program.

LITERATURE

Bible studies, Bible story telling, Scripture reading, and memory work fall into the category of literature art. Bible literature, used in this way in the camp setting, helps to integrate the spiritual into the total camp program.

Another literature area that should be explored is the use of good books. Good literature can be enjoyed during rest periods while the counselor or a camper reads from an interesting and exciting missionary biography or Christian novel. Campers enjoy listening to good literature. Reading may help in the discipline problems of these quieter times. A good camp library is an asset.

GRAPHICS

Campers can be exposed to challenging areas of expression through drawing and painting, using pencil sketching, charcoal, chalk, watercolors, oil, and acrylics. A very exciting program is that of photography. Making available simple cameras, camps may encourage campers to take black and white pictures and then develop, enlarge, and display their work.

In all areas of the camp art program there is great opportunity for carry-over. Many campers have recognized a skill and interest in some area of the arts and have continued to develop it. Camp is an ideal place for introducing campers to the arts and helping them to develop skill levels.

TYPES OF CRAFTS IN THE CAMP SETTING

Campcrafts are usually categorized in four major areas.

STANDARDIZED, COMMERCIAL PROJECTS

The standardized craft projects range from commercially packaged leathercraft kits, tooling projects, and jewelry kits to the supplying of various materials with patterns and designs to follow. A large number of projects are available commercially, and many books are available to give patterns and designs. Thus an effective program in standardized craft projects can be developed with either some research or the purchase of commercial packages.

This type of craft, a traditional approach in centralized programs, is more often used in conference or church school camping. Frequently, highly skilled personnel are available to oversee the various projects available to campers. These same projects are commercially available to campers when they go home. Ideas and materials can be evaluated by visiting craft stores or obtaining catalogs from craft companies.

NATURECRAFTS

Projects termed *naturecrafts* use the element of nature in and around the camp area and are more often used in decentralized programming. The emphasis is on creative expression in naturecrafts. Such programs also provide opportunity to teach respect for nature and the out-of-doors. While the actual carry-over of naturecraft is dependent upon the availability of nature-type materials, the awareness of the environment promoted in a naturecraft program provides considerable carry-over value. The emphasis should be on the use of natural supplies and material. Even an inner-city camper can use sticks, stones, paper, cloth, and other items from his environment when he returns home.

NATURE STUDY

The actual study of nature has more potential than is used by most camps. The Scriptures indicate that God makes Himself plain through our understanding and viewing of nature (Rom. 1:20). We should, therefore, increase our study of God's nature. There are two approaches:

1. *The "content knowledge" approach.* Here the names, descriptions, and recognition of various items in nature are stressed. This is usually more acceptable to those campers who are deeply interested in science and nature. A danger lies in making the nature study program too similar to a school experience. Campers may lose interest.

2. *The "sensual awareness" approach.* This implies meaningful observation of nature's sights, smells, and sounds. With this approach interest is usually well maintained, as camps successfully involve their campers in a deeper awareness of God's creation. A deep respect for the creative process and the Genesis account of Creation is often a direct result.

PRACTICAL CRAFTS AREA

Practical campcrafts are outdoor living skills taught at camp. This would include fire building, cooking, the setting up of camp, and survival in the out-of-doors. Knotcraft and lashing could also be included. These should involve the camper directly rather than through demonstration only.

Points to Consider in an Arts and Crafts Program

Arts and crafts do not just happen in camp. There must be a plan for the implementation of a program and the commitment to a quality program that benefits the camper and enhances the camp ministry. These are some basic considerations.

THE PROGRAM MUST BE COORDINATED

A coordinator must oversee the supplies and materials. His responsibilities include ordering and collecting materials. Likewise, a central work area should be maintained so that campers and cabin groups can have access to projects and supplies. Excitement may lead to neglect in cleaning up and putting away the materials and equipment. Someone must see that cleanup takes place. Someone should always oversee the craft program activities.

Expense must be kept in mind. This is especially true where commercial kits and standardized crafts projects are used. Some expense is involved even in the naturecraft program, although to a lesser degree. Some camps charge additionally for the use of supplies.

THE TIME AVAILABLE IS IMPORTANT

Short-term projects that can be completed fairly quickly provide the best opportunities for success, especially if craft time is optional. Long-term projects can be done but are more difficult and usually involve more skill. These can sometimes be conducted as group projects by cabins or special interest groups.

COUNSELOR ATTITUDE MUST BE CONSIDERED

Counselors may view the arts and crafts time entirely as a break for them. But counselors need to be with their campers to lend support in spiritual matters. Campers and counselors can often talk informally about some problem while working on a project. Counselors should be encouraged to use this valuable time in the camp ministry.

BASIC LISTINGS OF CRAFT PROJECTS

LEATHERCRAFT

Working with leather is one of the most popular of the standardized and commercial crafts. It varies from simple kits that call for a lacing with plastic or leather strips to completely tooled projects that require working of the leather with designs or lettering.

PLASTIC LACING

A popular craft project is plastic lacing. The lacing is available on large spools to camps. Projects include key ring chains, bracelets, belts, and lanyards. This enjoyable project is relatively inexpensive.

PLASTER MOLD PAINTING

Various molds of figures and plaques are available for plaster casting. Water-base colors should be provided to paint the castings. A complete project would require campers to mix plaster, pour the molds, release the plaster from the molds, and then paint the castings. A number of molds with religious themes are available. These fit well into the Christian camp setting.

DECOUPAGE

Decoupage, which involves coating pictures on a wood base, is relatively simple and can be used by even the youngest camper. Once the wood backing is selected, and the picture is applied, varnish-type finishes are alternated with careful sanding. Advanced skills in decoupage involve additional sanding and finishes. Again, a number of religious scenes, Bible verses, and writings are available to make decoupage particularly suited to church camp use.

INDIANCRAFT

Making Indian items fits well into the camp setting. The activity might include the use of leather, feathers, and beadwork. This very popular craft program ties into an Indian or Western camp theme.

NATURECRAFTS

Naturecrafts are highly creative. These projects allow the camper to express himself through combining nature and Christian themes. A listing of some of the more creative and interesting naturecrafts follows. Many books that would extend the list are available.

Collage. Probably the simplest of all the naturecrafts is the collage. This is a textured picture using elements of nature such as leaves, branches, twigs, stones, or whatever is available. The items are glued to an appropriate backing. The collage may have a particular meaning, be abstract, or actually be a scene.

Nature prints. Another popular item is nature prints. There are a number of ways to make such prints, and details can be found in the craft books of the Resources section. The prints are very beautiful, easily done, and include smoke prints, Ozlid prints, crayon or charcoal prints, spatter painting, and block printing.

Plaster of paris. A versatile item used in naturecraft is plaster of paris. This item can be used in a number of ways to involve the camper in nature and related areas. Sand-casting is one example. The campers make designs in sand, then pour plaster into the design. Plaster can also be used as a background for a collage. Plaster can be sculptured. Painting the hardened plaster adds to the enjoyment of the project. Casting of animal tracks is a favorite activity.

Whittling. Whittling is a very beneficial activity. Tools may be a simple jackknife or actual woodworking tools. Instruction in the proper use of whittling tools must be given to prevent injury. The tendency is to attempt projects that are too complicated, but there is an element of learning patience and creative expression in the carving of wood, soap, or plaster.

CRAFTS FOR NATURE STUDY

The study of nature can be approached in a number of ways, as the camp setting provides many opportunities to study God's creation. A formal biology or botany course is not recommended for camp however. Emphasis should be placed on awareness of nature and the relationship of man to his environment. The camp setting provides opportunity to observe the food chain, the oxygen cycle, and the progressions of weather. A realistic approach to nature is the "sense awareness" program which provides opportunity for the camper to become aware of the outdoors—to see, hear, and feel his environment and to learn his place in God's creation. Projects and a variety of programs in nature study will provide interest for most campers.

Terrarium. As a simple craft project, the terrarium is good for nature study. Almost any transparent glass container will work well. Some black dirt from an appropriate area in camp, some moss from an old log in the woods, a small fern, some grasses, little flowers, rocks, pebbles, and pieces of wood can be arranged to make a delightful project. If the camper wants to include small animals in the terrarium, be sure that the animals are released after a few hours. Insects, spiders, and earthworms are interesting creatures to include in the terrarium and can be kept a day or two before being released. One caution: there must be constant supervision of the terrarium projects to prevent glass breakage and possible injury. If the terrarium is tightly closed, a weather cycle can be observed. The terrarium will keep for months with little additional care.

Specimen dissection. There is sometimes interest in dissecting dead creatures found in the camp environment. Under competent leadership this can be a learning experience. Simple cutting tools might be obtained, and a dissecting pan is very helpful. Specimens that are most easily acquired are fish or small mammals found on the camp property. Large crayfish are unique and can be an interesting study.

New materials. Two new approaches have been developed for use in nature study programs in schools and camps.

The Outdoor Biology Instruction Strategies (OBIS) offers many creative ways of studying nature. One good craft project is the construction of tools to use in nature study. Plans are included in a kit. The OBIS material is of very high quality. Workshops are held at various times during the year in different parts of the country to provide experience in the use of OBIS materials.

Acclimatization is another new approach that attempts to involve the camper in a direct confrontation with nature. It encourages experienced campers to see their environment as the creatures of nature do.

CAMPERCRAFT

An effective camp program should include campercrafts. There should be exposure to the experience of living without conveniences in the outdoors. The campercraft program will teach and prepare the camper for these experiences.

For this type of program to be most effective, the staff should have thorough precamp training in the various aspects of campercraft. Elements of this training should include: setting up camp, outdoor cooking, and safety. A camping trip should be included in each precamp training period.

Fire Building. Instructions should be given concerning the types of fires, and how they are used in camp. Discussions of wood and its burning qualities are helpful. Safety is an essential factor in any instruction in fire building, and thorough respect for fire should be taught during this time.

Knotcraft. Counselors should know ten to fifteen knots that will be useful in the camp program. These will be valuable on the waterfront as well as in campcraft training. Instruction in this area should include the value of knotcraft, and how the knots are used. Lashing projects should be encouraged.

Outdoor cooking. This term means more than hamburgers and hot dogs. Other desirable, and tasteful items can easily be cooked outside. As a general rule, almost anything that is cooked in the kitchen can be cooked out-of-doors, although usually more time is needed in outdoor cooking. Breakfast is often very simple to do. After a night of sleeping outside, an appropriate breakfast cooked over an open fire can be the highlight of a camping trip.

Experiments in the various types of cooking for camping out may include cooking with foil, a variety of toasting methods, dutch oven cooking, pit cooking, and the common pan frying.

MATERIALS AVAILABLE FOR CAMP ARTS AND CRAFTS

In addition to resources listed at the end of this chapter, the following sources for ideas and materials are suggested.

LOCAL SCHOOLS AND COLLEGES

Teachers in the science and art departments of high schools and colleges are often interested in the development of good camp art and craft programs. These professionals will spend time helping and giving ideas for projects and resources. Evaluate their suggestions to be sure the projects can be completed in a short camp session.

COUNTY EXTENSION DEPARTMENTS AND 4-H PROGRAMS

County agents are very involved in arts and crafts and take a practical approach to crafts. They are on the public payroll to provide services. Extension departments have resource booklets and pamphlets available on a variety of craft projects. They are inexpensive and can be adapted to many camp programs.

COUNTY AND MUNICIPAL PARK DISTRICTS

A sizable amount of research has been done in environmental education and recreation. Nature programs are available through park districts of counties and larger cities. A library may be available for camp use. Some of the departments publish instructions for effective camp projects and nature study programs that they developed. Also, take time to participate in their programs. Many nature centers make staff people available for training or demonstrations.

GOVERNMENT AGENCIES—FEDERAL AND STATE

The United States Department of Health, Education, and Welfare has a number of materials available. These may be obtained from the Superintendent of Documents, Washington, D.C. Large metropolitan areas often have offices of this agency. Check with the United States Government Information Center for locations of these departments. State offices should be contacted at state capitals. Contact state environmental agencies for services and information.

COMMERCIAL CRAFT HOUSES AND STORES

Available craft projects can be viewed by catalog or in stores located in larger cities. Large craft franchises are available. The managers of these stores are open to discussing craft projects and may hold classes in crafts of interest.

CAMPING ASSOCIATIONS

Christian Camping International and American Camping Association provide training programs, conferences, and workshops in arts and crafts. Membership in these organizations and their local chapters will give exposure to many areas of camping and to arts and crafts in particular. These professional organizations are important resources.

SUMMARY

Achieving an effective camp arts and crafts program is work, but the benefits are outstanding. In few other ways can a camper and a counselor work together so closely. The counselor has tremendous opportunities to share and to grow with the camper through arts and crafts. The camper will take many memories and attitudes home from camp. Through an effective arts and craft program, he can have a greater understanding of himself, his relationship to God and others, and his relationship to his environment.

SUGGESTIONS FOR STUDY

1. Develop a basic statement on the place of arts and crafts in a Christian camp as it might be placed in a camp manual.
2. Draw up specific plans for a camp library. Recommend books for various age levels.
3. Write a thorough job description for a camp arts and crafts director.
4. From your knowledge of a particular camp, set up a nature study craft program for juniors.
5. Actually use one or more of the resources suggested under "Materials Available for Camp Arts and Crafts" on page 106.

RESOURCES

Bale, R. O. *Creative Nature Crafts*. Minneapolis, Minn.: Burgess, 1959.

Benson, Kenneth, and Frankson, Carl. *Creative Nature Crafts*. Englewood Cliffs, N.J.: Prentice-Hall, 1968.

Epple, Anne Orth. *Start Off in Nature Crafts*. Radnor, Pa.: Chilton, 1974.

Griggs, Patricia. *Creative Activities in Church Education*. Livermore, Calif.: Griggs Educational Serv., 1974.

Hammett, Catherine T. *Your Own Book of Campcraft*. New York: Pocket, 1950.

Hennepin County Park Reserve District. *Nature Crafts, Games, Activities, and Projects*. Excelsior, Minn.: Lowry Nature Center, n.d.

Hennepin County Park Reserve District. *Working with Children in the Outdoors*. Excelsior, Minn.: Lowry Nature Center, n.d.

Thomas, Dian. *Roughing It Easy*. Provo, Utah: Brigham Young U., 1974.

Tillman, Albert. *The Program Book for Recreational Professionals*. Palo Alto, Calif.: Mayfield, 1973.

van der Smissen, Betty, and Goering, Oswald. *A Leader's Guide to Nature-Oriented Activities*. 2d ed., Ames, Iowa: Iowa State U., 1968.

Van Matre, Steve. *Acclimatization*. Martinsville, Ind.: ACA, 1972.

Wilson, Gertrude, and Ryland, Gladys. *Social Group Work Practice*. Cambridge, Mass.: Houghton Mifflin, 1949.

———. *Outdoor Biology Instructional Strategies Set I*. Berkeley, Calif.: U. of California, 1975.

———. *Outdoor Biology Instructional Strategies Set II*. Berkeley, Calif.: U. of California, 1975.

7

Specialized Programs

P. Richard Bunger

- *Family Camping*
- *Day Camping*
- *Mobile Camping*
- *Special Purpose Camping*

P. RICHARD BUNGER(M.R.E., Fuller Theological Seminary) is executive director, Family Retreat and Resource Center of the Rockies, Englewood, Colorado. He has served as a member of the Camp Management Committee of the Conservative Baptist Association of Southern California.

In the mid-forties, camping specialists such as Raymond R. Peters were predicting, "A variety of camping experiments will be projected. We have not yet exhausted all the resources in the camping movement. In many ways the camping movement is still in its infancy."[1]

Where Christian camping is defined by rigidly traditional forms of meetings, schedules, and camper image, such development is, of course, considerably limited.

If, however, we establish our Christian camping purpose and use this as the basis for our camp ministry, then Peters's projection becomes quite valid. Leaders who have approached specialized camping programs on this basis have become involved in productive camping experiences. Patterns for effective programs can usually be found where the purpose is pointed toward meeting specialized needs.

While there are basic camp program principles, and some programming material can be used in almost any camp setting, the specialized type of camps have their own program needs. These are briefly discussed for the *family camp*, *day camp*, *mobile camp*, and *special purpose/interest* camp.

FAMILY CAMPING

Many authorities agree that the family finding time occasionally to be together in an area away from space-age pressures is an increasing necessity for the achievement of healthy family relations. It is here that family camping offers a rich ministry.

---

1. Raymond R. Peters, *Let's Go Camping* (Elgin, Ill.: Brethren Pub. House, 1945), p. 99.

MAJOR TYPES

One type of family camping is done on a graded or semi-graded basis. Here the family goes to facilities where activity programs are designed for each member at his own age level, but where the family lives and eats together. The schedule is coordinated to allow the family substantial time together. The camping facilities can be provided by an established camp, or, as in many denominational family camps, each family provides its own trailer or motor home. Likewise, eating facilities are flexible.

According to *Let's Go Camping* by Raymond R. Peters, these camps "make it possible for all age groups to come to camp at the same time. . . . The basic philosophy and objectives are similar to those in a regular graded camp. Some activities . . . are planned for all age groups, others on the various age levels. In some groups there is a common dining hall while in others each family provides its own meals."[2]

A second type of family camp is the one "in which the family as such is the primary administrative and program unit. The program majors in enrichment of family life and the improvement of family relationships. It includes many elements found in other camps such as the natural rustic setting, the vocational purpose and the personal enrichment experience."[3]

BENEFITS TO CONSIDER

According to Ed Branch, writing in *Marriage and Family Enrichment*, "The Family Camp is a *way of shifting gear* out of the workaday television watching, meaningless humdrum into which we may find ourselves slipping. It is an opportunity to try out a more dynamic family life. . . . A Family Camp keeps us with our family group so that one or two of us are not doing some changing that might come as an unpleasant shock to others. . . . Since the changes that might occur in the Family Camp occur with all the family members present, the behaviors should have a better chance of being carried back home."[4]

Speakers and workshop leaders who deal with Christian family life can share knowledge in a more relaxed atmosphere. The camp atmosphere provides immediate opportunity to practice what has

2. Ibid., pp. 34-35.
3. Ibid., p. 34.
4. Herbert A. Otto, ed., *Marriage and Family Enrichment* (Nashville: Abingdon, 1976), p. 51.

been taught. Self-awareness as well as biblical patterns for family life are encountered by all family members at the same time. The individuals who make up the family learn to live more effectively with members of their family as well as with other families.

The "cluster" of families in such a program has great value. Camping requires *cooperative living*. Jobs are shared—children's recreation, baby-sitting, perhaps cooking—adding interest to family learning. Parents learn from other parents through comparisons and observations which can be many times more effective than formalized instruction in family life or even counselor guidance. Family living apart from the stresses and problems of daily life reinforce knowledge gained from the more formal sessions.

PLANNING OBJECTIVES

Russell and June Wilson in discussing the "Family Enrichment Weekend" have listed assumptions and practical objectives which could as well be applied to family camping. The value of objectives is emphasized by the Wilsons: "We don't want to just go to camp and goof around and have recreation; we've done that. We would like to have some growing experience with our children."[5] Lloyd D. Mattson in *Family Camping; Handbook for Parents* strongly underscores this concept.[6]

Thus, a basic objective would be to provide an enjoyable family experience within the context of spiritual emphasis related to everyday living. The goal is to have the kind of experience that will strengthen the family and reinforce a positive image of the family for both parent and child. This could include the development of new communication skills and, for many, a new experience of affirming one another. The Wilsons state, for example, "Family members observe other families relating warmly and authentically without apology, and are affirmed in that behavior."[7]

FACILITIES

What type of facilities are needed for family camping? Branch feels that formal family camp facilities are not necessary for a good family camp experience. "Many families today have a tent, tent-

---

5. Ibid., pp. 44-45; 39.
6. Lloyd D. Mattson, *Family Camping; Handbook for Parents* (Chicago: Moody, 1973).
7. Russell L. Wilson, *Leaders Manual, Family Enrichment Weekend* (Russell L. Wilson, 1973), p. 3.

trailer or camper of some type which they are only too happy to use for sleeping accomodations."[8] Camps in the past have often majored in dormitory arrangements and gang-type restrooms. Such facilities do not lend themselves comfortably to a family emphasis. Facilities with large bedrooms (or smaller adjacent rooms) and companion baths are ideal. Even more ideal are separate cabins for each family. However, according to Robert P. Davis in *Church Camping*, the critical factor is "Housing of families must be as family units, with each having its own privacy for sleeping, dressing, family discussions and devotions."[9]

An important consideration is the eating arrangement. For example, kitchen accomodations within rooms or cabins might add to the frustrations of a family and just transplant home pressures to the camp setting. Branch emphasizes the value of including meal costs in the camp fee. Then, "no one has to interrupt . . . participation in order to prepare or clean up food."[10]

Care must be taken, of course, to see that a program is not priced out of the market. At the same time it may be necessary to educate prospective camping families by explaining the validity and importance of such a ministry. It also will be helpful to compare costs with that of general family vacations.

Finally, facilities should provide, or at least be adjacent to, areas where the family can find recreation together, such as hiking, boating, swimming, fishing, bicycling, backpacking, rafting, canoeing, horseback riding, and crafts.

Day Camping

According to the American Camping Association's definition, organized day camping is "an experience in group living in a natural environment. It is sustained experience carried on in the daytime under the supervision of trained leadership."[11] A day camping program allows the camper to participate during the day and then return home in the evening.

Robert P. Davis quotes Maude Dryden, considered by many to be the leading voice of the day camp movement, as noting, "Day Camping is such a flexible plan that a variation of it can be suited to

---

8. Otto, p. 52.
9. Robert Pickens Davis, *Church Camping* (Richmond: John Knox, 1969), p. 59.
10. Otto, p. 52
11. *Standards Report for the Accreditation of Organized Camps* (Martinsville, Ind.: ACA, 1966), p. 7.

almost any condition, always being based on its principle function, that of leading back to simple leavening pleasures of the woods and streams and blue skies."[12]

Though there can be wide variations, according to Clarice Bowman in *Spiritual Values in Camping*, "Day camp functions from six to eight hours per day, with campers having only the noon meals at the camp. Some are conducted for one, two, or three days a week. Programs may resemble those of resident camps. Campers may be brought together to a site in a forest preserve, in a park, on a beach, on a farm or on a specialized camp site. Because of their accessibility to the camper's home, day camps are not limited to summer."[13]

VALUES

Day camping is more than just preparation for resident camping, although this may be part of its value. Originally such camping was designed for elementary children who were not yet ready to be away from home for prolonged periods or even overnight. Day camping has special value where resident camping cannot be experienced because of lack of available camps or limited finances.

The value of individuals working together in small groups can be found in the day camp experience. Davis notes that a day camp program provides the following:

1. opportunity to foster Christian growth
2. opportunity to express the church's concern for the individual
3. opportunity to have freedom of space, actions, and expression outside of a classroom situation
4. opportunity for self-understanding as well as for development of relationships with peers and leaders on a consistent basis
5. opportunity to have a more exciting kind of learning environment
6. opportunity to find a lasting fellowship on which other learning experiences can be built
7. opportunity for evangelistic outreach that would include some who could not be reached any other way
8. opportunity for elimination of the status symbol of clothing, as camp attire is usually very casual.[14]

---

12. Davis, p. 42.
13. Clarice Bowman, *Spiritual Values In Camping* (New York: Association, 1954), p. 12.
14. Davis, p. 46.

PROGRAM

If the day camp serves as a continuation of the regular church educational program, curriculum materials may be those ordinarily used. If additional curriculum is needed, vacation Bible school material often can be utilized. Nature-oriented crafts can usually be included. Virginia Musselman's *Day Camp Program Book* is helpful.[15] Another possibility is a modified approach to the resident camp program.

FACILITIES

The facilities required for a day camp are relatively few: readily available drinking water, toilet and hand washing facilities, refuse disposal, and, ideally, a fireplace. Some type of shelter is helpful. This need not be a permanent structure; a tent or any covered area to provide shade and protection from rain or wind will serve. The location of the facilities in relationship to the campers is important. Davis suggests a practical maximum travel time of forty-five to sixty minutes.

Equipment requirements are fewer than in resident camping. The imagination and resourcefulness of the leader along with the natural resources of the site will guide in the selection of program equipment.

MOBILE CAMPING

A specialized form of camping that is rapidly growing in popularity, especially with youth, is that which involves travel. Chapter 3 discussed the two major types of camping, resident and nonresident programs. Nonresident camping includes day camps and mobile programs.

TRAVEL CAMPS

Mobile camps utilizing motorized vehicles are labeled *travel camps*. Family camping caravans and missionary youth caravans are examples. While the values of such programs are evident, they have not at this point become a major part of the Christian camping movement.

---

15. Virginia Musselman, *Day Camp Program Book* (New York: Association, 1963).

TRIP CAMPS

Mobile camps moving by nonmotorized means are identified as *trip camps*. These include bicycle trips, canoe and kayak trips, backpacking, horse pack trips, and combinations of hiking and packing with animals. One author says the purpose of this type of camping "is to bring about the individual's Christian growth within a Christian community, rather than *just* to cover space or see beautiful or historic sites."[16]

Trip camping is usually planned for high school youth, though junior and junior high youth can benefit from trip camps of one- or two-day duration. Younger campers often are not physically or emotionally equipped to handle the extended, more demanding trip.

A primary value of trip-camp experience grows out of the training and preparation necessary. The process of such preparation develops a kind of self-directed discipline. Another valuable dimension of trip camping is the community life that develops. Building interdependent relationships essential to wilderness travel and then living comfortably within the relational framework is basic to all of life.

Obviously, permanent facilities are of minor importance to trip camping; however, good dependable *equipment* is vital. Adequate planning and preparation are the keys to success. The mode of transportation must be thoroughly understood by all participants.

A bicycle trip, for example, requires backup equipment and spare parts to prevent delays. Extra wheels, tires, and other vulnerable parts must be on hand.

Campers should be trained to manage minor repairs on their own bicycles. Safety and riding instructions must be ingrained.

Space and weight of supplies must be well calculated, and each individual must accept his share of the total load. Personal discipline on the part of campers includes both physical and emotional factors as difficult days are encountered. Study sessions prior to a trip are important for a thorough understanding of the geographical areas to be covered and problems that might arise. Advance training is essential for such areas as handling canoes or horses.

Bicycle or canoe trips where towns are occasionally encountered differ substantially from wilderness trips in that supplies can be purchased along the way. The wilderness traveler has only what planning and preparation have provided in his pack.

The cost of special clothing and camping gear should be weighed as trip camp expenses are projected. Poor gear just won't do! An

---

16. Davis, p. 48.

equipment breakdown experienced by one camper can spoil the trip for the entire party.

Two contrasting approaches to the wilderness experience are the trail camp and the stress camp. Though the setting may be identical, the objectives differ widely. Wilderness trail camping approaches outdoor living as a major goal in itself, along with the spiritual objectives common to all Christian camping.

Certainly education belongs in the list of wilderness goals. Every camper should be exposed to as many useful ideas as possible. His store of campcraft and woodlore would be enriched, not through formal instruction but through personal experience. Yet the overriding goal for all Christian education is the growth of the spirit. The unbiblical, sacred-secular dichotomy has wrought irreparable damage to some Christians. The wilderness provides a laboratory in Christian living, demonstrating that the Spirit of Christ pervades every area of life, and every relationship.[17]

Trail camping seeks the adventure of the wilderness unfolding day by day. Trail camping success is achieved when the camper learns to keep warm, dry, and well fed regardless of weather or trail difficulties. The initiative and discipline required for comfortable living on the trail introduce campers to a world of discovery. To relate the adventure of the Christ-life to the adventure of the wilderness experience is the expressed objective of one organization specializing in wilderness and stress camping.[18]

Trail camping includes a wide variety of wilderness sports and skills. One organization, for example, offers canoeing, backpacking, rock-climbing, orienteering, mountaineering, and ice-climbing seminars; plus skiing, snowshoeing, dog sledding, and winter outdoor camping.[19]

People today are concerned about nature values. The wilderness

17. Lloyd D. Mattson, *The Wilderness Way* (Cotton, Minn.: Whiteface Woods, 1970), p. 16.
18. Christian High Adventure, 201 S. Third, Montrose, Colo., 81401. This is a joint ministry of the Special Mission Ministries Department of the Home Mission Board, Southern Baptist Convention; the Recreation Department of the Sunday School Board of the Southern Baptist Convention; and the Brotherhood Commission.
19. Adventurous Christians, Gunflint Star Route, Grand Marais, Minn., 55604.

can be enjoyed and utilized as a teaching medium. The wilderness offers a tremendous opportunity to find a close, practical walk with a personal God for "since the creation of the world His invisible attributes, His eternal power and divine nature, have been clearly seen, being understood through what has been made" (Rom. 1:19-20).

WILDERNESS STRESS CAMP

The stress camp differs from the trail camp in its objectives and somewhat in its program. While the goals of trail camping include the aim that a camper will learn how to live comfortably with minimal gear, the wilderness stress camp adds another dimension: growth through physical and mental stress.

Stressful situations are deliberately created to test the camper beyond his normal endurance. The wilderness sports of whitewater canoeing and kayaking, technical rock climbing, and rappelling often form part of the curriculum. These teach the critical necessity for teamwork and trust.

As the trail camp moves, it follows practical trails. The stress camp, however, may lead its campers through a swamp or up the face of a cliff. Trail camps normally operate programs not exceeding ten days' duration. The true stress camp requires several weeks just to condition campers physically and mentally for the ordeals that must be faced.

The origin of the term *stress* in relation to this form of mobile camping is difficult to trace. (Some sponsors call their programs *hard-core camping*.) The best known of this kind of training camp are the Outward Bound Schools, which have grown rapidly since the early sixties. Outward Bound sponsors schools in Minnesota, Oregon, Maine, Colorado, and North Carolina. These provide 26-day training sessions.

A feature commonly found in stress camping is the *solo*, a two- or three-day experience that finds the camper totally alone, living as much as possible off the land.

Stress camping has been incorporated into the programs of several Christian camping organizations. Wheaton College, Wheaton, Illinois, for example, sponsors a Vanguard camp, one of the oldest and most highly developed wilderness stress programs incorporating spiritual objectives.

Stress camping demands sensitive, highly skilled leadership, for there are physical and psychological dangers. Lacking adequate preparation and training, campers may readily be injured or psychologically damaged. Given competent leadership, the wilderness stress camp provides young people with growth experiences rarely matched in any other area of life.

Just as resident camping now functions throughout the year, so mobile camps remain active year-round. Wilderness survival snow camps are growing in popularity. Campers take to the trails on skis or snowshoes; they live in tents or snow caves. The values gained through personally confronting the rigors of nature build a spiritual stamina into the camper. "In a mysterious way one's sense of security seems to involve his identity with these basics (necessities of life: food, shelter, clothing, transportation). Somewhere in man's spirit there is a need for participation, not merely buying or observing life."[20]

SPECIAL PURPOSE CAMPING

Clarice Bowman points out: "Special purpose programs are adapted to particular groups of campers such as older adults, handicapped children, persons with health problems and the like."[21] In addition, special interests such as aquatics, art, conservation, athletics, dramatics, language, mass communication, music, ranching, Christian education teacher training, or even technical skills are often the basis for camp organization.

The pattern of group living in an outdoor setting over an extended period of time that we call camping can serve an almost unlimited variety of special needs. Where facilities allow, the often-neglected handicapped or disadvantaged person can gain many of the values camping offers the rest of society. Living with peers helps handicapped persons grow in dimensions many times overlooked in the home community where most people are not handicapped. There is challenging camping ministry here for blind and deaf, mentally retarded, and other handicapped persons.

Camps for special persons require carefully trained personnel and facilities suited to the needs of the handicapped. Many camps now are redesigning old buildings and including in plans for new structures the features required to serve wheelchair campers and those with other types of limitations.

Specialized programs of camping are a continuing challenge for the Christian camp leader who seeks to minister through camping to people of many interests and needs. As a specialized camp is developed, it should be planned around the individual camper's (1)

20. Mattson, *The Wilderness Way*, p. 5.
21. Bowman, p. 13.

abilities—whether limited or developing, (2) interests—whether expressed or latent, and (3) needs—whether physical or mental.

SUGGESTIONS FOR STUDY

1. Do you agree or disagree with Raymond Peter's statement regarding camping infancy? Why? Be prepared to defend your position.
2. Look through several Christian magazines and notice the kinds of camps that are advertised. Catagorize under the different types of camps listed in this chapter, noting age limits and costs.
3. On the basis of ideas set forth in this chapter regarding family camping, discuss with another member of the class and then list the kinds of changes that can be made in families through the camping experience.
4. How would you go about determining the needs of individuals in a day camp program?
5. Write out your personal view of the kinds of travel camps that are practical. List the values of each.
6. What is your view of wilderness trip or stress camping in relation to valid camping principles?
7. Contrast the program objectives of the wilderness trip camp and the stress camp.
8. List what you feel are the strengths and weaknesses of travel camps and trip camps when compared with resident camping in regard to the potential for fulfilling spiritual objectives.
9. What factors limit the capability of a camp to serve special interest campers?

RESOURCES

Basic materials are indicated in the footnotes.

Training Programs: A Case Study
Wesley E. Harty

Christian camping is considerably broader than fire building in the outdoors. As a tool in making disciples, it offers a wide potential in the training of men, women, and youth. To indicate some of this potential, we have included this chapter as a case study of what one camp ministry has done. Forest Home in Southern California, a pioneer in Christian camping, has been long known for its innovative programs such as Indian Teepee Village for junior campers.

EDITORS

WESLEY E. HARTY (B.A., Westmont College) is Coordinator of Publicity and Promotion at Forest Home Christian Conference Center (Calif.) and active in various leadership positions at Forest Home, including that of registrar and supervisor of Indian Village.
Note: As a case study, this chapter does not include suggestions for study or resource listing.

- *CILTS–Camper-In-Leadership-Training*
- *Youth Corps*
- *AIDs–Assistants in Day Camping*
- *Camping Education*
- *Adult Training Programs*

If to Shakespeare all the world's a stage, to those in Christian camping the whole out-of-doors is a classroom. Henrietta Mears, founder of Forest Home Christian Conference Center, constantly emphasized the use of the "teachable moments" scattered through the camp day from flag raising to taps. She encouraged counselors and leaders to take advantage of the smallest event or circumstance that could be used to teach God's truth.

Thus the camp setting becomes a natural classroom. The time can be structured so that teaching and learning go on in a way not possible at school or in the local church.

To use the camp context for special training, two guidelines need to be kept in mind. Can the training be done better in the special milieu of camping than in the local church, home, or school? And is it possible to conduct the training only in camp? As a rule these two criteria have been the focus maintained by Forest Home in the development of programs and projects beyond the usual activities of a conference center. There is no need merely to duplicate what has been done at home. Look at the camp, its facilities, its resources and staff, and see where it provides a special ministry opportunity.

The areas to be discussed in this chapter are programs that have taken root and flowered in the special soil of Forest Home. The principles out of which they have been established are valid. However, each camp must seek not merely to imitate or duplicate but to adapt, or refine, or perhaps create something new.

The two longest-running training programs at Forest Home are the CILTS and the Youth Corps (more popularly known as the "Blue Helmets"). Both programs were begun in the early 1960s and have since proved their intrinsic value.

CILTS—CAMPER-IN-LEADERSHIP TRAINING

Camper-in-Leadership Training is not a junior counselor program. It is a four/five week intensive session in teaching, counseling, and small group activities, intended to do just what it says: train for leadership. When CILT was initiated, it was open to young men and women going into their junior or senior year of high school. Now it is also offered to entering college freshmen.

The training includes Bible study, leadership concepts, and counseling, not just in theory but also in actual practice. CILT young people learn principles of Bible study, then have the chance to exercise them in living situations among their own peers as well as in the stretching experience of counseling juniors or perhaps junior highs for a week. They not only read and discuss material on counseling (such as H. Norman Wright's *Help! I'm a Camp Counselor*)[1], but they work for six days in the give-and-take of camping with an active group of fourth, fifth, and sixth graders, or a questioning, seeking gang of seventh and eighth graders.

The camp in essence becomes a learning, experience-centered laboratory. CILTS theorize, define, and evaluate, but then they get a vital opportunity to work out the concepts and succeed—or fail. In counseling, the CILT is assigned to an experienced lead counselor and also carefully supervised by the CILT director.

Behind the counseling, the Bible study, and the devotions lies a constant emphasis on true Christian leadership. One of the most important goals of the CILT sessions is to develop the young person not just for four weeks at Forest Home but to assume a responsible role in his church and school. One of the thrilling things over the years has been to see graduates of CILT rise to the challenge of the program and return home to take up fruitful positions of leadership in secular student bodies and church youth groups.

A major portion of the CILT program is what is sometimes known as *body life*. The four or five weeks at Forest Home is not only a living experience, it is a living-together-working-together-struggling-together experience. Participants in the program are housed in units away from the main center of camp. An old cabin has been turned into a meeting room and lounge. Meals are taken (except when counseling or backpacking) with the summer staff in the dining room.

Outside of the basic rules of the conference center and general rules set up by the CILT director, the guidelines for living are established by the young people. They then become responsible for helping one another live within these guidelines and rules. The sixteen or twenty of them form into committees and learn not only to make plans but also to carry them to a conclusion. Whether a backpacking trip or a Bible study is being organized, the young people develop very practical aspects of being both leaders and followers.

---

1. H. Norman Wright, *Help! I'm a Camp Counselor* (Glendale, Calif.: Regal, 1968).

Another area of inestimable value to each CILT is an assignment of several days' duration in some practical department of Forest Home: registration, food service, accommodations, or maintenance. This provides an excellent opportunity to see the day-to-day administration of a camping program while working closely with those whose job it is to keep a conference center functioning. What makes the activity doubly valuable is the evaluation each CILT must do on his work experience, and the evaluation the department head must submit on the CILT. Often the youth discovers strengths he never knew he had or weaknesses he had never dealt with.

How does a young person get into the program? First he or she contacts Forest Home and receives a number of forms: a comprehensive application-personal information sheet and three reference blanks which must be filled out by competent adults who know the person. When this material is returned and processed, and final acceptance is determined by Forest Home leadership, the applicant is notified of acceptance, conditioned upon the final step, a physical examination by his family doctor.

YOUTH CORPS

For most of the summer around the grounds of Forest Home one will see the ubiquitous blue helmet—the badge of a Youth Corps boy. As the aim of CILT is leadership training, the goal of the Corps is development and discipline, morally, spiritually, and physically.

Youth Corps is open to boys going into their last three years of high school. The young men must apply, be evaluated, and be accepted by the Corps leaders. The demanding five weeks place strong emphasis on stress training that builds muscles, emotions, and endurance.

The first week often proves to be the most difficult of the five. During that week the Corps coaches set up the rules and lay down the law. Within those first days a boy either decides to stick it out, or finds the pace just too demanding and opts for going home— something few have done over the years.

After six days, the young man who has held up under the rigors of the first week receives his blue helmet. He is now a full-fledged member of the Youth Corps and proudly wears that helmet everywhere as he continues his training for another four weeks.

The key factor in selecting projects for the boys is the concept of meaningful labor. Never are these projects merely busywork. What corpsmen engage in must be of value to them and must in some way help them enhance the setting and therefore the ministry of Forest

Home. To this day one of the most beautiful spots at the conference center is the Sermon on the Mount Chapel by Lake Mears. The Youth Corps, under the supervision of a landscape architect, labored all one summer, gathering and positioning rocks, laying out paths, and clearing the grounds to make a setting that would heighten the loveliness of the chapel knoll. Corpsmen have returned years later, now married and with children, to point out the boulders they were responsible for moving.

Besides physical labor there is time each day for guided weight lifting and weight training. As the program progresses it becomes very evident that emphasis is laid upon both stress and stretching—and upon the self-discipline needed to meet the daily challenges.

What makes the Corps unique is the concern of the coaches not only for the physical but also for the spiritual growth of the individual young man. Boys are encouraged in their own Bible study, and they learn to lead others in study of the Word. Quiet time alone with the Lord becomes an essential part of the Corps sessions, as does group and personal counseling. In keeping with the discipling purpose of camping as projected in chapter 1, the youth camp leaders (coaches) are a key to the program success. These men have not been the kind to stand back and declare, "Do as I say." They rather walk daily beside their boys or just slightly ahead, proclaiming by life and word, "Follow me." This is true even when discipline must now and then be exacted. It is not at all unusual to see a boy running an extra mile because of some infraction of Youth Corps rules—and to see his coach in stride with him all the way.

The final training each summer is a backpack into the San Gorgonio Wilderness, thirty-eight thousand acres of rough mountain terrain adjacent to Forest Home. Much of what has been learned about living and working as a body is put into practice during the four days in the back country. The boys are responsible for planning and carrying out the camping and the cooking. The challenge of the week is to reach the top of Mount San Bernardino, the 10,426-foot peak that overshadows Forest Home, and then move on to Mount San Gorgonio, the highest mountain in Southern California (11,500 feet).

AIDs—Assistants in Day Camping

On a shorter-range basis, AIDs is one of the best on-the-job training projects at Forest Home.

Over the years, the ministry to families at Forest Home has grown in both size and number. Now seven out of eleven summer weeks at the conference center are devoted to family conferences. But if such conferences are to be truly effective, young children need to be cared for and taught while parents are in adult sessions. So along with the development of day camp programs has come AIDs.

Each week thirty to forty teenagers come to camp specifically to assist in the children's work. These young people make application, submit references, and then pay ten dollars for the privilege of serving their Lord by caring for young children.

Essentially the program runs as follows: the AIDs are divided into two groups. Each young person is assigned to work with the age level of his or her choice (toddlers, preschoolers, primaries) as far as possible. During the morning hours, Group 1 works with the youngsters while Group 2 is in a Bible study and training session taught by the adult supervisors. The training covers such areas as age group characteristics, children's recreation and games, storytelling, and elementary first aid. Midway through the morning, the groups of AIDs reverse, so that all spend time both at work and in instruction.

The number of AIDs is determined by the number of children eight years and under present at each conference. The ratio runs about one AID for every three children.

The young people have more than morning day camp responsibilities. After dinner in the evenings, AIDs are assigned to families for whom they will babysit. Fifteen minutes prior to the adults' evening inspirational hour, AIDs arrive at the family cabins and from then until 10:30 P.M. take care of the children. AIDs' counselors make regular checks on the AIDs during these hours to ensure adequate adult supervision the entire time the young people are on duty.

Conference is not all work and no play. Afternoons are open for AIDs to use the lake or the pool or to relax at the recreational facilities available for all conferees.

What the day camping and AIDs program does is put parents at ease throughout their week at Forest Home. They know their children are well cared for, morning and evening. Because of this, mothers and fathers are more open to the ministry of the Word and the Holy Spirit and more apt to participate in and enjoy the activities planned for them.

AIDs have become an invaluable asset to family camping at Forest Home. Now even weekend conferences in October and those held over the Thanksgiving and Memorial Day holidays feature full-scale child-care programs.

CAMPING EDUCATION

The ministry of a conference center must cut two ways: outward toward its conferees and inward toward its student staff. The staff's spiritual and professional growth must be an active concern of the administrative staff. Chapel services, group Bible studies, and personal counseling are all aids to that growth and development.

At Forest Home an additional area of that ministry to staff has been the camping education class. Working with Westmont College of Santa Barbara, California, and under the supervision of a Westmont College faculty member, the Forest Home Christian Conference Center offers credit for an eight-week course in Christian camping. The credit, granted by Westmont, is transferable to the student's own college in the areas of physical education, education, or Christian education.

The major thrust behind the program is to make available to summer staffers an opportunity to study, discuss, observe, and participate in practical camping procedures and activities, all within academic guidelines: in short, to be employed and at the same time to receive college credit.

In the first year or two of the program, the Westmont professor spent ten weeks setting up the class, directing it, and personally supervising each student. Eventually one of the Forest Home permanent staffers was certified by the college, and the professor was only on the grounds at the beginning and closing of the eight weeks.

Basic text for the course was *Camp Counseling*[2] by A. Viola Mitchell, Ida B. Crawford, and Julia D. Robberson. One year Jay Adam's *Competent to Counsel*[3] was a companion text. Fundamental to the course was the instruction by Forest Home leadership and the use of the camp setting as a practical laboratory for study and observation.

Class discussions covered such areas as the philosophy and objectives of Christian camping, the science of outdoors programming, the counselor's role and relationships, techniques of discipline, needs and problems of the camper, forest hazards, and safety tips. Each class time featured a camping professional or, if available, one of the conference speakers having expertise germane to the course of study.

---

2. A. Viola Mitchell, Ida B. Crawford, and Julia D. Robberson, *Camp Counseling*, 4th ed., (Philadelphia: Saunders, 1970).
3. Jay Edward Adams, *Competent to Counsel* (Nutley, N.J.: Pres. and Ref. Pub., 1970).

ADULT TRAINING PROGRAMS

Many people consider camp as a training setting for youth only. However, a camp program especially geared to adults for a particular area of training or growth has tremendous potential.

Can it be done better in camp than in the church or school? Without question the three programs about to be discussed could be conducted elsewhere; however, the added ingredient of living-together-learning-together-eating-together for a week or a weekend plus informal interaction with the leadership over an extended period of time make the conference center an ideal place for adult training projects.

During summer family weeks, Forest Home offers optional seminars on family devotions and how to lead a Bible study. But three specialized conferences—Executive/Management, Church Lay Leadership, and Christian Writers—are conducted each year for the specific purpose of adult leadership training.

EXECUTIVE/MANAGEMENT CONFERENCE

The first Forest Home Executive/Management conference, held in 1975, was begun at the request of a Christian business executive. He felt the need for a retreat to which Christian men and women in executive positions could invite friends in comparable positions and all be exposed to motivational seminars having a clear emphasis on Christ in the life of a business leader.

Getting the right speaker for this sort of conference is crucial. First of all he must be someone successful in the business world; he must have earned the right to address those in his profession. Then he must exhibit a working, growing relationship with Jesus Christ, so that the challenge comes across from a life as well as from principles.

CHURCH LAY LEADERS

A guiding philosophy of Forest Home, since its inception, has been that the conference center should be the camping arm of the local church. In the spirit of that philosophy, the Church Lay Leaders weekend was developed in 1975.

Many lay people are elected to church office without really knowing the requirements that devolve on men and women in leadership positions. The Lay Leaders Conference came into being not to tell deacons or deaconesses of their specific roles but to expose them to certain principles of leadership and to how leadership may be carried out within the local church.

Each conference has featured a pastor who knows how to work with his lay leaders and who understands the New Testament concept and purpose of the church. In addition to the pastor-layperson relationship, great stress is placed on biblical principles and priorities of leadership, goal setting (both personal and congregational), leaders as servants, and developing patterns of cooperation between leaders and the groups they represent in the local church.

Great emphasis is laid on reading. Each lay leader is given a book list, prepared cooperatively by the visiting pastor and the conference staff, that includes such material as *Be the Leader You Were Meant to Be*, by LeRoy Eims;[4] *Motivation and Leadership*, a cassette album by Dr. Howard Hendricks;[5] *The Church: The Body of Christ*, John MacArthur;[6] and *Design for Discipleship*, J. Dwight Pentecost.[7]

CHRISTIAN WRITERS

The aim of the four-day Christian Writers Conference is to "challenge Christian writers to express their basic loyalty to Jesus Christ, and to implement their desires to bear dynamic witness to Him through the finest possible use of the English language." So stated the first publicity brochure sent out in the winter of 1971. As consistently as possible, those goals have been adhered to.

The titles of some of the seminars and sessions give a good idea of the thrust of the four days: "Common Mistakes of Beginning Writers," "What Editors Can't Resist," "The Bible Teaching Article," and "Writing for Children (or Teens or Adults)". Applicants are asked to submit a two-hundred-word theme on a subject of their own choosing. Those who are finally selected need not be published authors, but they do need to be serious about the challenge of Christian literature and their desire to produce quality work that could be considered for publication.

4. LeRoy Eims, *Be the Leader You Were Meant to Be* (Wheaton, Ill.: Victor, 1975).
5. This cassette was produced in 1970 by Campus Crusade for Christ, Int., Arrowhead Springs, San Bernardino, Calif. 92414.
6. John MacArthur, *The Church: The Body of Christ* (Grand Rapids: Zondervan, 1973).
7. J. Dwight Pentecost, *Design for Discipleship* (Grand Rapids: Zondervan, 1971).

Unit 3

Christian Camp Staffing

The purpose and program of the first two units—no matter how ideally they may be projected—must inevitably come for fulfillment to the subject of this unit, staffing. Here is both the underlying dynamic of the strong camp and the continuing struggle of the weak.

The opening chapter in the unit surveys the *camp staff positions*, noting qualifications and responsibilities. Both program and counselor staff for normal camp operation are considered.

A dynamic camp staff does not just happen—it is built by sound *recruiting and training* practices. It is maintained by planned follow-up programs. These are the areas covered in the second chapter.

The essential focus of an effective staff is on *the camper*, and each staff person shares in the opportunity of contributing to his personal growth. This work with campers is deepened by our understanding of the camper, and there is a unit chapter on the characteristics and development of each of the four major children-youth age groups.

The final chapter in the unit takes us through a study of just how and when we can work with the camper in the camp setting. The wide range of *counseling* opportunities is another exciting commentary on the versatility of the camping experience.

Staffing in the Christian camp is considerably more than a matter of providing live bodies. As a discipler, the Christian staff member has a uniquely challenging ministry, as Wesley R. Willis, Harold J. Westing, Joy Mackay, and J. Omar Brubaker carefully portray.

9

Staff Personnel

Wesley R. Willis

- *Program Staff*
- *Counselor Staff*

One of the tasks of greatest concern to quality-oriented camp boards, and justifiably so, is the building of a competent program-counseling staff. Camp staff and camp philosophy have a dynamic,

WESLEY R. WILLIS (Ed. D., Indiana University) is academic dean, Fort Wayne Bible College, Fort Wayne, Indiana. Dr. Willis has been active in camp leadership, especially wilderness experiences. He teaches camping courses at Fort Wayne Bible College.

crucial relationship. On one hand, a staff with no coherent camp philosophy to guide it will be limited in effectiveness and diverse in operation. But likewise, a camp philosophy without the proper staff to implement it is theoretical at best.

While normal camp staffing allows for certain flexibility in recruitment and duties, there are of course guidelines and established principles in camp operational policies. There must be standards. If, for example, by *Christian* camp we mean one that provides a total life experience that enables more mature Christians to disciple less mature Christians, then the Christian camp is immediately confronted with the absolute necessity of staffing with mature, committed, Christian men and women.

In addition to its status as Christian, the camp must likewise be a valid *camping* experience. There is, therefore, the strong implication that the out-of-doors, or nature, will have a significant influence on the program, either as the context in which certain activities take place or as emphasizing God's natural creation as an integral part of all program activities. In either case, the staff must understand, be comfortable in, and truly enjoy the outdoor environment. Furthermore, since nature and natural revelation play a significant part in God's communication to mankind, staff members must have sufficient theological understanding to enable them to achieve a genuine biblical perspective of nature and ecology.

But also, in seeking to achieve a working relationship between available staff and established program, there must be room for adjustment. Thus, the program director will normally plan a tentative program for the coming season and then seek the ideal personnel to staff that program. It is important, however, to maintain flexibility so that when the completely ideal staff is not secured, the program plans can be modified to take advantage of the unique qualities inherent among the persons available.

PROGRAM STAFF

Naturally, the size of the camp will determine the actual number and composition of the program staff. However, the administrative structure suggested here is adaptable and can effectively accommodate a variety of camp sizes. There are four leadership levels, plus another category whose exact development will depend on the operating philosophy of the camp.

The program staff has basic administrative responsibility for camp activities and personnel.

The *director* is responsible for the overall operation of the camp.

The *program director* reports to the director and is responsible for all aspects of program. A *unit director* (sometimes called *head counselor*) supervises the work of a group of *counselors*. The *activity specialists* are individuals who will instruct in specialized areas such as riflery, waterfront, and the like. In some cases the activity specialists may be counselors, or they may be hired specifically for particular instructional skills. A suggested organizational chart of the program area can be seen in the following illustration:

DIRECTOR

Qualifications. The camp director should preferably be a minimum of thirty years of age and hold a college level degree from a recognized educational institution. The degree ideally should be in the field of camping or business administration, with possibly a minor in the alternate field. The director must have a keen understanding of business and management principles and be especially competent in interpersonal relationships. He must be a mature Christian with basic biblical and theological training. He should have substantial experience in a variety of camp leadership positions, preferably with at least two years of experience in a counseling or specialist responsibility and at least two years in a second level management position (program director or business manager).

Responsibilities. The camp director is responsible for the overall operation of the camp. This means coordinating all levels of camp leadership (see diagram) and representing them to the camp board, to whom he is directly responsible. He will assist the camp board in the determination of policy and will present to the board recommendations for major expenditures and the hiring of administrative personnel.

It is important that the camp director recognize responsibility for working with the camp board in camp philosophy and the policies to be followed in implementing that philosophy. The director bears responsibility to interpret board action to the administrative personnel reporting to him and to assist them in the effective carrying out of camp policy. It is the director who will assure the smooth, consistent operation of a camp. To that end he will encourage maximum contribution from both the camp board to whom he reports and the personnel reporting to him.

PROGRAM DIRECTOR

Qualifications. The program director should be a minimum of twenty-five years of age and hold a college level degree from a recognized educational instituion. The degree ideally should be in camping or recreational leadership. He should also have basic biblical and theological training. The program director needs skill in interpersonal relationships and communication and should have several years of successful experience in camp leadership, including counselor and unit director work.

Responsibilities. The program director oversees and guides the effective operation of the camp program. This includes training, supervising, and assisting program personnel. The program director works with the camp director in the development of policy and reports directly to him.

Since the position includes the responsibility for a program that is both effective and safe, this person must be an alert, well-trained individual. And because a camp's spiritual ministry is an integral part of the total camp program, a part of the program director's duty is to inspire and guide his program staff to design and take advantage of spiritual teaching opportunities in all areas of activity.

UNIT DIRECTOR (HEAD COUNSELOR, CAMP DEAN)

Qualifications. The unit director should be at least twenty-one years of age and either a college graduate or within one year of graduation. He should have several years of experience in camping, two of them in a counseling position. This person must be sensitive to the needs and feelings of the counselors. The unit director may also possess specialist skills that will complement the contribution of other staff in the camp program.

Responsiblities. In a decentralized camp using camper units, or small groups, the unit director is responsible for a camper pattern that ordinarily consists of four counselors. In a more centralized type of organization, a head counselor works with all the counselors. The unit director helps the counselors plan and implement the unit program as well as assisting them with difficult camper problems. Since camps will vary in size, any organizational pattern must include flexibility. This is especially true where a unit type of organization is used. Thus, in the very small camp there may be only one or two unit leaders. In some cases the program director may even serve as a unit director, although this should be avoided in all but the smallest camps. In a very large camp there could be as many as ten or twelve unit directors.

SPECIALISTS

The specialized skills of a wide variety of individuals can be incorporated into the camp program. The philosophy of a camp will help

determine the role that specialists play. In a totally decentralized approach, for example, the instruction in special skills may well be handled in the cabin units and taught by the counselors. In a more centralized camp, the counselors may have more limited responsibilities, and the campers may spend part of each day in other groupings where they will learn under the guidance of a specialist. In some cases, the counselor may work with a cabin group for part of each day and as a skill specialist with a different group for another part of the daily program.

The number and kind of specialists employed will naturally be determined by each camp's facilities and objectives. A caution should be given at this point: no camp can be all things to all people. Some activities that will be incorporated naturally into one camp's program would be very difficult to fit into another's. The determination of a camp philosophy and consistent operating policies is prerequisite to deciding which activities to include. A list of the specialties offered in some camps includes the following:

Archery	Orienteering (map and compass)
Arts and crafts	Riflery
Backpacking	Rock climbing
Boating (power/rowing)	Sailing
Canoeing	Spelunking (cave exploration)
Conservation	Sports
Horsemanship	Swimming
Life saving	Tripping (hiking, biking)
Nature lore	Wilderness living

It is critically important that specialists provide adequate leadership in the areas where the health and safety of the campers are at stake. Most camp programs include swimming and other waterfront activities. Due to potential water hazard there must be a competent water safety instructor in charge. Another especially critical area is riflery. Although the qualifications for all specialists will not be given, the following two are representative of the type of qualifications to be sought in the skill areas.

WATERFRONT DIRECTOR

Qualifications. The waterfront director should be a minimum of twenty-one years of age and hold a Red Cross Water Safety Instructor rating. This person should have several years of camping experience with at least one year of experience in waterfront activity.

Responsibilities. The waterfront director is responsible for encouraging the establishment of recognized waterfront safety procedures and supervising their consistent implementation. His recommendations should be made to the program director, to whom the waterfront director is ordinarily responsible. The waterfront director oversees all waterfront activities including swimming, boating, canoeing, and any other water specialties offered by the camp. Other leaders in water activities report to him. There should be a minimum of one counselor on duty for every ten campers on the waterfront at any given time.

RIFLERY INSTRUCTOR

Qualifications. An instructor in riflery should be a minimum of twenty-one years old and be competent in shooting skill as well as teaching skill. An instructor should hold the National Rifle Association Instructor rating or its equivalent. This person should have several years of experience in camping; at least one of these should have been in a leadership position.

Responsibilities. The instructor should be responsible for recommending safety procedures and guidelines and assuring their consistent implementation. The responsiblity for the storage of equipment and supplies as well as for the supervision of their use should be included. The riflery instructor should evaluate the supplies needed, both before and during camp, and assume responsibility to requisition the purchase of supplies well before they are exhausted. As in all specialty areas, the instructor is responsible for maintaining the good condition of the equipment through proper cleaning and maintenance and for recommending any replacement or addition needed.

Counselor Staff

IMPORTANCE

Of all the camp personnel, many feel the counselor is in the most strategic position. There are two basic reasons for this.

First, whether the camp leans toward the centralized or the decentralized approach, the counselor is the one personally relating to the camper. He lives with the camper and will likely be the one to whom the camper goes with questions or problems. While there may be an excellent speaker in a centralized camp, the counselor will probably still do much of the in-depth counseling. In a decentralized camp, the counselor is all the more strategic, since the counselor is the one who has the major contacts with the campers.

The second reason the counselor is strategic is that it is the counselor who interprets camp philosophy to the camper. Most Christian camps believe every individual is important to God, that God has answers to young people's problems, and that young people can be helped to discover and develop their potential through meaningful exposure to a natural environment. It is the counselor who helps the camper learn this and apply the principles to his life.

A camp may have a well-formulated philosophy written out in its by-laws. The director may understand the dynamics of relationships between people cooperating to live comfortably in a wilderness context. However, such concepts never get off paper and into campers' lives until the counselor guides them in practical interpretation.[1]

QUALIFICATIONS

A counselor should be eighteen years of age at the minimum, and it is recommended that at least half of the staff be twenty-one or older. Several years of personal camping experience, including one year as a junior counselor, are desirable. If the counselor is also expected to instruct in a skill, there must be adequate qualification in that area as well.

In addition to basic qualifications, it is imperative to seek counselors with desired, but realistic, personal qualities. There are job descriptions whose standards suggest a counselor with the wisdom of Solomon, the patience of Job, the eating habits of John the Baptist, the musical and athletic skills of David, the elocution of Apol-

---

1. Where a camp has a discipleship purpose, it is the counselor who becomes the basic discipler.

los, the aggressiveness of Peter, and the theological understanding of Paul!

There are three realistic attributes to look for when recruiting counselors:

Spiritual maturity and sensitivity. Since the counselor has most of the direct ministry to campers, spiritual maturity is crucial. The immature counselor will be preoccupied with personal problems and not be able or available to help campers with their problems. The immature counselor will break down under the constant scrutiny of the camper who wants to know if Jesus Christ really does make a difference in a Christian's life.

Spiritual maturity involves the ability to take the concepts and principles of the Word of God and consistently apply them to everyday situations. It means that spiritual personal habit patterns have been established. In 1 Timothy 3:6 Paul admonishes Timothy not to place a novice in a position of spiritual leadership but to seek a person who has demonstrated spiritual consistency. The ideal counselor is one who is accustomed to relying upon the power of God and who responds to situations with a spontaneous spirituality.

Hebrews 5 indicates that spiritual maturity includes not only an awareness enabling one to discern good and evil but also the ability to take what is known and share it with others in a teaching context. Probably the best way to describe the ideal counselor is as a discipler—one who is guiding another into the application of spiritual truth to life, even as others have guided that counselor.

The spiritually sensitive counselor will see where a camper has needs and be prepared to guide him in applying God's Word to the problem at hand.

Personal relationship skills. Spiritual maturity and relating to people are inseparable. When one reads about the fruit of the Spirit (Gal. 5:22-26), it becomes obvious that spirituality correlates with human relationships.

A good counselor loves people. But this means an active, outgoing love and not merely the ability to verbalize how concerned one is. Counselors are going to find that they will be "on call," in many cases, twenty-four hours a day.

Skills in personal relationships demand discovering *why* the camper acts like that instead of reacting to *what* was done. It means taking time to listen and discover how a camper feels inside rather than being ready with an answer before the question is asked.

There was, for example, the camper who seemed to have his own black cloud. If a window was broken, he was near it. If there was a disturbance at campfire, the counselors knew who was in the middle of it. When they saw him coming, they expected trouble. Finally out of desperation, a unit director took him off alone and discovered that he had become a Christian three weeks ago and that his father had gone to prison the previous Friday! Everyone had been so busy trying to keep him in line that no one had taken time to relate to him as a person.

Skills in personal relationships demand a genuine interest in other people, and time and ability to communicate with them. This involves listening as well as talking.

Technical camping skills. Certain skills can be taught to a counselor in precamp training, but ideally a counselor has previously developed skills in living in the out-of-doors.

All-around campcraft skills become essential in the more decentralized camp. As totally decentralized, a trail camp demands a broad range of skills and wilderness competency. Not only must the comfort and enjoyment of the campers be considered but also their safety and, possibly, even survival.

Strengths in one skill area may balance some weakness in another, but it must be remembered that a camp program will be no stronger than the counselors. The goal in recruitment is a counselor who is strong in each of the three areas diagrammed below.

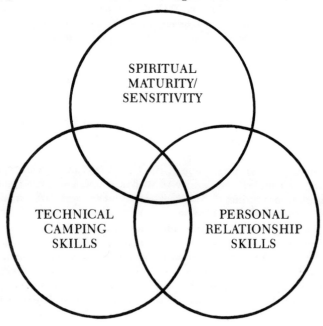

RESPONSIBILITIES

A counselor is responsible for the direct supervision of the six to twelve campers assigned to his cabin.[2] Each cabin group will have, preferably, a junior counselor to assist the counselor. In a strongly decentralized camp, the counselor will have major responsibility for his campers, including Bible teaching and certain skill instruction. In a more centralized camp, the counselor's responsibliity is supervising assigned campers during specific periods of time, including rest and sleep periods. With this type program, counselors may have additional responsibilities such as skill instruction or waterfront counseling. The philosophy and operating policies of a camp will determine the actual job description and specific responsibilities of a counselor.

Due to the strategic nature of the counseling position, it would be well to examine further the matter of responsibilities. As has been suggested, the counselor is the strategic connecting link in the administrator-counselor-camper chain.

In this regard, the basic responsibilities of the counselor can be summarized under the headings of supervision, instruction, and guidance.

Supervision. The counselor must help insure adequate rest, safety in activities, and participation in program. Through it all there is opportunity to build discipling relationships. Supervision is a significant ministry as well as a critical responsibility.

Instruction. From the centralized approach where a counselor may concentrate on teaching one or two skills to the decentralized emphasis where he teaches total living and survival, instruction plays a key role. Whether a counselor teaches Bible to a cabin group

---

2. For a full discussion of the counselor carrying out his responsibilities, see chapter 12, "Camp Counseling: Working with Campers."

or participates in informal discussion following centralized instruction, a counselor will be instructing.

Basic to the teaching responsibility is the need for clear understanding of just what is expected of the counselor and thorough preparation as well, including guidance in how to teach effectively. Christian camping affords an opportunity to demonstrate how spiritual principles relate to and can influence *all* aspects of a person's being.

Guidance. The diagram below illustrates ideal spiritual development. Jesus Christ at the center of one's life should be expanding into and influencing all dimensions of personality.

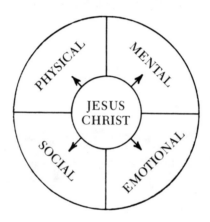

The counselor should be ready to guide the camper in such application of spiritual emphasis. Whether it be the decision to accept Christ or to receive God's help in dealing with an uncontrolled temper, the counselor's guidance is strategic.

Counselors are the heart of a camp ministry and should be chosen with great care. They should be spiritually mature, possess good interpersonal relationship skills, and have basic camping knowledge.

SUGGESTIONS FOR STUDY

1. Why can the counselor be called the key link in the camp personnel structure?
2. List the basic positions in program staff and the minimum ages recommended for each position.
3. What qualities should be sought in recruiting counselors? Why are these strategic?
4. Describe the interrelationship between spirituality and the component elements of personality.
5. What is the relationship between a camp philosophy and the task of staffing? In what ways is each dependent on the other? In what way does each modify the other?
6. Design a series of counselor Bible studies that could be used in a camp. These should provide study questions and discussion guides.
7. After personal study, compile a list of Bible passages that will help the counselor deal with problems in the physical, mental, social, and emotional dimensions.
8. Design a form on which you could record the observations made in a counselor interview. This should provide easy access to your conclusions.
9. Do an in-depth study of the qualifications of a spiritual leader as described by Paul in 1 Timothy 3:1-13. Be sure to compile a list of these, taken from a contemporary translation that is faithful to the original Greek. How could this be used with your program staff?
10. Based on your personal philosophy of Christian camping, draw up a counselor job description that would include the tasks of all counselors, as well as those responsibilities that would be unique to your camp.

RESOURCES

Hartwig, Marie, and Myers, Bettye. *Children Are Human*. 4 vols. Minneapolis: Burgess, 1961-63.

How to Be a Camp Counselor. Wheaton, Ill.: Scripture Press, 1967.

Ledlie, John A., and Holbein, F. W. *Camp Counselor's Manual*. New York: Association, 1958.

Mackay, Joy. *Creative Camping*. Wheaton, Ill.: Victor, 1977.

————. *Raindrops Keep Falling on My Tent*. Wheaton, Ill.: Scripture Press, 1972.

Mattson, Lloyd D. *Foul-Up or Follow-Up?* Wheaton, Ill.: Scripture Press, 1974.

————. *Way to Grow*. Wheaton, Ill.: Scripture Press, 1973.

Mitchell, A. Viola; Crawford, Ida B.; and Robberson, Julia D. *Camp Counseling*. 4th ed. Philadelphia: Saunders, 1970.

Todd, Floyd, and Todd, Pauline. *Camping for Christian Youth*. New York: Harper & Row. 1963.

Wright, H. Norman. *Help! I'm a Camp Counselor*. Glendale, Calif.: Regal, 1968.

YOUTH Camp Director's Safety Guide. Washington: National Safety Council, 1972.

Counselor

(Applicant's name)

Camp Staff Application
Attachment #1

SPECIALIZATION/EXPERIENCE

Special training:_____

Length of time of training: _____

Experience as a camper (years and places) _____

With what age group(s) do you work best? _____

In the following list, mark a 1 by those activities you could organize and teach, mark a 2 by those you could assist in teaching, and a 3 by those with which you are slightly familiar:

GROUP ACTIVITIES
___ Bible Study
___ Campfire programs
___ Skits and stunts
___ Large group games and competition, treasure hunts, etc.
___ other: _____

SPORTS
___ Archery
___ Badminton
___ Riding (horsemanship)
___ Riding (bicycling)
___ Riflery
___ Softball
___ Field Hockey
___ Tennis
___ Volleyball
___ other: _____

SWIMMING (check classification)—
___ Advanced
___ Intermediate
___ Beginner
___ Non-swimmer

NATURE ACTIVITIES
___ Animals
___ Astronomy
___ Birds
___ Ecology
___ Forestry
___ Insects
___ Plants (identification)
___ Plants (edible)
___ Rocks and minerals
___ Weather
___ Bible lessons from nature
___ other: _____

WATERFRONT
___ Canoeing
___ Water Skiing
___ Diving
___ Lifesaving (WSI)
___ Sailing
___ Swimming
___ Water carnival activities
___ other: _____

WILDERNESS & STRESS CAMPING
___ Camping (tent/wilderness/overnight)
___ Fishing
___ Canoeing
___ Rafting
___ Repelling
___ Hiking
___ Outdoor cooking
___ other:_____

MUSIC
___ Lead singing
___ Play guitar
___ play _____
___ play _____

CRAFTS
___ Macrame
___ Weaving
___ Lacing
___ Candle making
___ clay modeling
___ Painting
___ Seed pictures
___ other: _____

10

Building the Camp Staff

Harold J. Westing

- *Recruiting the Staff*
- *Training the Staff*
- *Coaching the Staff*

You are talking with a junior boy as he unloads his suitcase and duffel bag onto his bunk at camp. His fishing pole, basketball, football, and Frisbee, along with the excitement written all over his face

HAROLD J. WESTING, (M.Div., Western Seminary, Portland) is associate professor of Christian education, Conservative Baptist Theological Seminary, Denver, Colorado. He has been camp director, Woodbine Ranch (Colo.) and Tadmor on the Mountain (Oreg.), and active as a CCI board member.

clearly indicate that he has come to camp for a good time. The luggage and paraphernalia a person brings to camp indicate that one of the major reasons for putting down money to spend a week at camp is the feeling that this is the place to have fun and adventure. Therefore, as you watch the load the junior boy is putting on his bunk, you are aware that *your* goals for the camper may be significantly different from his.

You are concerned that in the midst of all the camp activity he will personally relate to Jesus Christ and that his knowledge and attitudes and values will consequently show change—change that is consistent with Scripture.

The challenge of camp, then, is to provide the adventure and excitement that a camper longs for but in the process develop genuine qualities of Christian character. How is this task to be accomplished? Luke 6:40 teaches us: "A student is not above his teacher, but everyone who is fully trained will be like his teacher" (NIV). This clearly written objective for Christian education indicates that as a camper is taught he is becoming like his counselor. It becomes apparent then that all personnel who are involved in providing a meaningful experience for the campers need to project the quality of life in Christ that we expect to see developed in campers' lives.

It is possible to provide spacious and expensive campgrounds and an ideal camp setting, yet fail to accomplish this biblical objective.

The one basic ingredient that makes the difference between a camp program that is simply interesting and fun and one that produces godliness in the lives of the students is the *quality of the life of the staff*. A camp manager and his board must give serious consideration to adequate facility and programming, but first priority should be given to adequate recruitment and training of staff who *can* communicate by the quality of their lives the likeness of Christ.

RECRUITING THE STAFF

No crash program of recruitment or training will adequately do the job that should have been accomplished over a period of time. People normally start thinking about camp in the spring, but an adequate recruitment program should begin at the end of the previous season. Meaningful contacts are made for recruiting future staff as older campers leave the grounds. Likewise you will be in touch with key workers from the current staff for the next season. Camp follow-up rallies also provide means for making contacts for the succeeding year's staff.

Although the camp manager and his personnel committee and board will make the final decisions, everyone acquainted with your camp is a potential recruiter for staff. There is wisdom in exposing all of your camp family, for example, to the various staff opportunities because of their contacts with possible personnel.

A *currently successful camp program* is a critical ingredient in effective recruiting. When a positive image is conveyed by your campers, people will come and often sacrifice to be a part of the staff. Normally, this kind of reputation takes time to build up. Another significant ingredient is *a dynamic and godly recruiter*. His personal involvement with people and churches, college campuses, youth rallies, and district association meetings will play a significant role in finding the personnel to build a dynamic staff.

The Christian service offices of Bible schools and colleges usually cooperate by establishing interviews for potential staff people on campus. Other campus personnel may provide opportunities for participation in classes and chapel services to give exposure to your camp and the available service opportunities it affords. Personal encounter with potential staff cannot be too strongly emphasized as one of the most meaningful ways of recruiting.

Do not overlook the importance of the material sent to your camp mailing list. This list should be made up of all previous campers, donors, pastors, and church staff persons in your area. The mailings should always apprise your readers of personnel needs and inform them how to make application for the positions. In all recruitment practices, of course, it should always be kept in mind that it is the Lord of the harvest who sends forth laborers into His harvest, including the Christian camp field. Thus, some camps recruit prayer bands who not only pray specifically for the needs of each week of camp but also play a significant role in praying for the recruitment of an adequate staff.

Many camp boards and directors never have enough applicants so that they can be selective. They are grateful to get any born again Christians who are willing to come and work on the camp staff. But often the problem of low quality staff also relates to inadequate application materials. Although no application or reference forms are foolproof, these are very important first steps in screening applicants for the various positions.

Every application will, of course, request basic autobiographical information about the applicant. Helpful in determining the quality of the person are insights into his past, including such items as his relationship with Christ in a local church and his work record. (Note his productivity and the quality of his involvement with other persons on the job.) An up-to-date record of the applicant's educational status will also give insight into the quality of his life. Information about musical, artistic, and athletic background will provide additional knowledge as to how this person can best serve in the camp program. Each applicant should be asked to furnish references, which might supply further insights.

TRAINING THE STAFF

The quality of the life of the staff is indeed the most important ingredient in developing an effective camp program. This fact provides a basic mandate for carefully training your entire staff—one of the most neglected practices in church camping.

Some directors reason that since they may have a volunteer staff, such workers should not be asked to take training. Yet, it has been shown that counselors are much quicker to volunteer when training is offered; also, they will develop a far greater appreciation and respect for their position and responsibility once they are adequately trained. It is extremely important to recognize that *both* voluntary and paid staff need to receive training if they are to aid in developing a quality camp.

Other camp directors sometimes feel that since their staff members come only for a week or two, they do not need to bother to train them. Again, there needs to be a reminder that the staff is the most vital ingredient in a high quality camp program, whether for a week or a whole summer.

Camp studies show that the cabin life and the one-to-one relationship with staff members are the factors contributing most to the personal growth of campers. Even in a centralized camping program, the life the counselor lives before the campers is one of the strongest influences in developing spiritual growth. Training *is* essential.

Some camps offer counselor training for only the first time a counselor goes to camp. Yet, the more one studies the science of counseling, the more one realizes that there must be ongoing training to strengthen and refresh the abilities of the staff to do quality work.

One criterion for successful training was well expressed by a Pioneer Girls staff member, Wilma Garrett, who suggests that training has not occurred for any particular person on the staff until he has replaced less effective behavior with more effective behavior in the performance of staff responsibilities. The camp administrator has the responsibility of implementing the training program. Each individual must be helped to actually modify his responses to some degree when he faces real life situations in the camping arena.

Besides regular training sessions, there are other ways to help the staff. Cathie Nicoll, director of Pioneer camps in British Columbia, *personally corresponds* with all of her counselors for the coming camping season. She uses this opportunity to establish a friendly relationship with them, as well as to prepare them spiritually and mentally for the task that lies ahead.

Having the counselors take a correspondence course is another effective way to prepare them for their assignments. A number of such courses are available (e.g., the Moody Correspondence School course).

A very practical training means is to have the staff read camp-related books. These could include books on camp counseling, camp programming, and personal evangelism, as well as the great spiritual classics.

Basic training, of course, is provided by well-planned training sessions. If the majority of the staff members live reasonably close to the campsite, you may want to have them on the grounds for some sessions during the year. Often training is done just before the actual start of camp. In the local church there can be a series of sessions on a weekend or on weekday evenings.

As you develop your training program you will want to give serious consideration to the desired outcome of the training time. A basic training program might include the following items:

1. History and background of your camp
2. The particular camp philosophy which your camp has developed and out of which you will be operating
3. Characteristics of a competent counselor
4. The philosophy of discipline
5. Counseling techniques that will be used in developing Christian character in your campers
6. Program concepts that will provide the rationale behind the agenda of the program
7. Place of music in the camp program
8. Local camp policies
9. Special training in each worker's specific responsibility
10. Clarification of the lines of authority so that each staff person will understand his line of accountability
11. The art and skill of leading a camper to Christ
12. How to use the Bible in the camp program: in the quiet time, camp devotions, campfires, personal counsel, and Bible study.

Helpful educational guidelines should be kept in mind as you develop your training program:

1. Both *generalization* (arriving at general principles applicable to many circumstances) and *transfer* (applying generalization learning in one setting to similar situations in different settings) are developed and encouraged in the training situation. You can see, therefore, the importance of having open discussion in training sessions for counselors to develop understanding of how general knowledge applies to specific instances. A grasp of this concept tends to provide a flexible, adaptable, and coping staff.

2. When a counselor *discovers for himself* some specific truth, he becomes less susceptible to memory loss and becomes more personally involved. Counselors will be much more excited about camp-related truth they learn from investigation and study than about that learned simply from a lecture.

3. Counselors have a strong tendency to perpetuate the kind of teaching they receive from the *models* around them in the training experience. Therefore, the style of training you provide will tend to become the kind of training they will provide for the campers who are under them. If you provide a discovery-type learning experience for your counselors, for example, they will tend to do the same for their campers. Consequently it is important that you demonstrate the kind of teaching skills that you trust your counselors and staff will use during their experience with the campers. Since Christian camping provides a testing laboratory for the total Christian life, it is important that a wide variety of learning experiences be used for the counselors in training. Give consideration to the following suggestions:

    a. *Visuals:* films, filmstrips, charts, chalkboards, models, displays
    b. *Participation:* projects, research, skill practice, assigned reading, discussion, trips (specifically, there could be living through a camping experience, nature field trips, developing craft projects, practice in outdoor cooking, sleep-outs, major hikes)
    c. *Other methods:* demonstration, seminars, buzz groups, lectures, role play, brainstorming, case studies, use of check list, psychodrama.

4. Training that is *personal* tends to have a far greater impact than that which is of a general nature. Consequently, some of the training program should be structured so that each staff member will receive some individualized instruction. During the training sessions you may want to have each trainee perform a particular skill he is learning.

5. Students learn as they are *stretched* mentally, physically, and emotionally. This will further emphasize the use of individualized training. One type of program will not necessarily stretch every individual. The schedule can be basically the same, but within that schedule there must be programming for each individual to grow in his respective area of study. Although review is profitable for last year's staff, it is very important that the repeat staff members be introduced to additional concepts in counseling so that the training course will stimulate them as well. Then, since much of the camp program involves physical exertion for the staff, it is also important that staff members be prepared physically so that they will not become fatigued during the regular camping season. This is done both by instruction in good health habits and the practice of these during training sessions.

COACHING THE STAFF

One of the most effective environments for training Christian leaders is the camp setting. It provides maximum opportunity for the leader or trainer to be constantly involved with the trainees. There are three main approaches to camp coaching, that is, using the camp setting as training opportunity.

COUNSELOR-IN-TRAINING PROGRAM

The counselor-in-training program allows potential counselors to spend time on the camp grounds learning from senior counselors as they model effective counseling. CIT people do not learn only from counselor models but have reading, study, and experiential assignments to amplify their learning. Some camps start with a student as early as the ninth grade, and the CIT program may extend as much as four years. The CIT plan, of course, assumes that the senior counselors have had adequate instruction and training, so that they will be able to properly guide the trainees.

The CIT, or junior counselor position, provides incentive for the older camper to become a leader. A CIT should neither be considered a flunky—simply someone who relieves the director of office-keeping duties—nor an assistant counselor to be saddled with routine assignments. He should have a demanding, high-level study course plus training in all the camp skills. The person who is the head of the CIT program will want to meet regularly with the trainees and guide them in the carefully planned training schedule. A good CIT program can develop a waiting list of counselors who know both your campsite and program first hand.

STAFF MEETING

A properly conducted camp staff meeting is an educational process and should demonstrate leadership techniques in positive fashion. The camp director will look on his staff meetings as more than opportunities to discuss the problems of the day. While problems are worked with and programs evaluated, the staff meeting provides a rich opportunity for developing that sense of oneness that enables the camp program to truly reflect the unity of Christ.

The trifles of the camp program should be taken care of by special committees of individuals who will work out the details. Nor is staff meeting a time for the camp director to deal with individual camp staff in relation to corrective measures. These should be taken care of in personal interviews with those involved.

The camp director will want to communicate to the staff the program procedures for the following hours and in so doing convey the rationale behind those programs. During the staff meeting, as time permits, he will give additional training in practical counseling procedures.

INDIVIDUAL CONFERENCES

A third approach to coaching the staff provides that a complete staff have a head or lead counselor who will work personally with each counselor to help with counseling problems and to encourage the counselor's personal growth. This person, of course, will need to be a spiritually warm, mature adult who can relate well to the rest of the camp staff. The counselors should feel free to express their fears, weaknesses, and hopes for good counseling, as well as be open to suggestions from the head counselor. A significant part of any individual conference will be the time spent together relating to the Word of God and praying for the counselor and campers involved. The lead counselor will want to spend some of his time observing the way each counselor leads a Bible study, directs an athletic event, or relates to his campers. Keep in mind that recognition and praise for good work is an essential part of good staff morale. Give it freely. It is a good idea, incidentally, to make clear to the staff the positive nature of the head counselor's availability and ministry.

There is a double reward for the director and management as they see counselors gain a rich and satisfying experience that is good equipment not only for camp but for a lifetime of Christian service.

Some camps provide special opportunity for individual counselors to develop their own spiritual life and character. Included is the giving of a personality test like the Taylor-Johnson Temperament Analysis (Psychological Publications, Inc., 5300 Hollywood Blvd., Los Angeles, CA 90027). Any camp that anticipates providing such service for counselors should, of course, have an adequately trained staff worker who can use such material.

SUGGESTIONS FOR STUDY

1. From the data in "Recruiting the Staff," develop an application form that you could use in recruiting staff.
2. Write out five key questions you might use to interview potential counselor candidates.
3. Develop a one-day's assignment you might use for a CIT as a lesson concerning cabin devotions.
4. Plan an agenda for a staff meeting that would deal with the current day's business plus one training item.
5. From the chapter, make a list of the characteristics you would hope to see in a senior counselor who would be responsible for training other counselors.

RESOURCES

Graendorf, Werner C., and Crosby, Jerry *Christian Camp Counseling Correspondence Course*. Chicago: Moody, 1979.
Johnson, L. Ted., and Kingsley, Lee M. *Blueprint for Quality*. Chicago: Harvest, 1969.
Mattson, Lloyd D. *Camping Guideposts*. Chicago: Moody, 1972.
Wright, H. Norman. *Help! I'm a Camp Counselor*. Glendale, Calif.: Regal, 1968.

11

Camp Counseling:
Understanding Campers

Joy Mackay

- *The Primary Camper*
- *The Junior Camper*
- *The Junior High Camper*
- *The High School Camper*

JOY MACKAY (M.A., Wheaton College) is professor of education, Central State University, Wilberforce, Ohio. She has directed Pioneer Girls camps and since 1959 has been associated with the Summer Institute of Camping, Word of Life (N.Y.). She is the author of *Creative Camping* and is the teacher of a camp course at Central State University.

Camp is for the camper!

You have heard this many times, but the words take on new meaning when you consider the role of the counselor. How successful the counselor becomes depends considerably on how well he or she understands the camper.

There are books about camper characteristics (see "Resources" at the end of this chapter), but remember that no boy or girl will be exactly like any example. Each camper is different from all others. A camper may be like a twelve-year-old physically, a fourteen-year-old mentally, act like a ten-year-old emotionally, and be a baby spiritually. Not one camper in the cabin may seem "average."

However, campers do have identifiable characteristics that help us understand them. Each age level has its own basic development, which provides guidance for the camp leader working with that age. We shall look, therefore, at general characteristics for the primary, junior, junior high, and senior high age levels.

But before considering the specific levels, it might be noted that there are general camper needs that affect all age levels.

1. The need for *security*. A camper needs to feel wanted. He needs a sense of belonging—to feel important in the cabin and in the camp.

2. The need for *recognition*. A camper wants to be recognized as an individual—not as camper number 197 in a camp of 400. The counselor should learn his name the first day, for using a camper's name is significant. It says, You matter. You are important in this camp.

3. The need for *new experiences*. Campers want to do in camp what they cannot do at home. Ideally we will leave at home, school, or church those activities that can be done just as well there and do in camp the distinctively camp activities. Primaries like surprises. Juniors like to be challenged by the new and different. Junior highs want a change from the commonplace, and senior highs thrive on excitement and daring. Camp, within the Christian framework and rules of safety, ought to provide these experiences.

4. The need for *involvement*—or a chance to make an investment of self. Particularly high schoolers want to give themselves to something bigger than they are. This is the strength of programs such as the Peace Corps and Vista. Camp should demand much of the teenager, thus giving him a sense of achievement and self-worth as he accepts difficult challenges. Camp can be a time of stretching physically, mentally, and spiritually.

The Primary Camper (Ages 6,7,8)

CHARACTERISTICS OF THE PRIMARY

At six, the primary's life is one of change and adjustment. He is no longer a little child. His world is widening from home and family to school or camp. His behavior may be extreme. He may seem awkward and clumsy as his body takes on new proportions. His eye-hand coordination is not too well developed. He has little emotional control. He is beginning peer activities and has to win his own acceptance in his world. He asks lots of questions. He has little concept of time and space. He thinks in terms of here and now. He enjoys the same stories over and over and enjoys acting them out. His interest span is short. The six-year-old's social consciousness is developing through his contacts in school, although he may try to make friends by teasing or hitting another child. Usually his best friend is one of the same sex. His attitudes can be greatly influenced by the example of a camp counselor.

At six, a child can pray and expect God to answer his prayers. He is capable of accepting Christ and can understand that He took his punishment in his place. He is literal minded and thinks in concrete terms. Teaching through Bible stories appeals to his great imagination. He can picture himself shipwrecked with Paul or marching with Joshua around Jericho. Symbolic and abstract terms should be avoided when working with primaries. Many children's choruses use symbolic language and are not ideally suited to children.

At seven years, a camper's growth has leveled off somewhat. His need for activity continues. He wiggles and squirms. He is developing manual dexterity. He has learned to print. He now daydreams and procrastinates. He is sensitive to the approval of adults. He is not usually satisfied with his craft project, but he will want the counselor to like it. He is still dependent upon adults but wants freedom. He tries to copy a favorite adult—many times this is his counselor.

The seven-year-old still loves stories and make-believe, although he does not always distinguish between the tale and the truth. Be sure he understands that Bible stories are true. He will enjoy a continued story at a campfire.

His attention span extends up to twenty minutes. He cares about what adults think of him, and to get a cabin cleaned, praise will go further than scolding. He is still somewhat self-centered. He generally trusts adults and can easily learn to trust God. His vocabulary is growing, and in many situations he has learned to fight with words instead of fists. He plays with others but wants to always win. To lose is hard, and he may not want to play that game again.

The camper at seven has developed patterns of getting along with others. Some of these patterns you will want to reinforce; others should be discouraged. He is developing his own concept of right and wrong. God's standard can become meaningful to him. He asks questions about heaven and God. He can show concern for the lost. If there has been a death in his family, he may want to talk about death.

He has a sense of awe and wonder about the world of nature and can be easily led into a worship experience as he sees the marvel of creation. He.needs to know about the beginning of life on the earth.

At eight years, a camper looks more mature. He wants to experiment and try out new things. He is able to take criticism from his peer group. He should become a good reader at this age. He can save money for some object he wants. He collects things, and trades. He likes to put on plays and even write his own scripts. He loves games. He may tend to be bossy, yet he respects authority.

DEVELOPMENTAL TASKS FOR THE PRIMARY—(areas where a counselor can help the camper)

He should be taking pride in his cabin.
He is developing a sense of personal worth.
He should develop a willingness to share.
He should feel secure and loved.
He is attempting to extend his own personality.
He can understand what is sin.
He can know sorrow for sin.
He may be ready to accept Christ as his personal Savior.
He should be learning to handle money and know its value. (With a counselor's help, purchasing at the camp trading post can become a learning experience.)
He is learning obedience to God as well as to his parents and others in authority.
He can learn Bible customs and background.
He can learn Christian stewardship.
He should memorize Scripture that is meaningful to him.
He should be able to relate the Bible to his everyday life.
He is learning to overcome unreasonable fears.
He can read silently and can be taught to have his own personal devotions.

THE JUNIOR CAMPER (ages 9,10,11)

CHARACTERISTICS OF THE JUNIOR

The junior age is a time of steady growth both physically and mentally; usually there are no sudden spurts. The junior is acting more independently of adults. Girls move one or two years ahead of boys in maturity.

A junior is active physically. He likes rough-and-tumble games and wrestling for their sheer action. He never walks when he can run, never opens a gate when he can jump over it, never walks on a sidewalk when he can test his balance on the fence. He rarely wants to clean the cabin or empty the waste can unless some competition is involved. He is always competing against himself or others. He likes to play with someone of his own sex. He is usually healthy at this age and loves camp and all its activities except rest hour and going to bed.

The junior camper can take care of his clothes, but boys usually do not care how they look. The counselor will need to see that the boys change underwear and put on clean shirts, or they will go home with a suitcase full of clean clothes.

Girls may not have the identical problem, but they may leave camp without sweaters, jackets, and Bibles.

The junior loves the out-of-doors. He loves camp, hiking, outdoor cooking, overnights, exploring, campfires, nature, fishing, sports, watercraft, swimming, and conservation. Camp, it seems, was made for a junior.

He is a collector. He collects rocks, stamps, nature specimens, baseball cards, gum wrappers—almost anything. The quality is not important; it is the quantity that counts. He is interested in many things, and collecting and comparing are ways of learning.

A junior camper is inquisitive. He wants to know why and how. He will sometimes stump the counselor with his questions.

He can memorize well. This is a good time to learn Scripture passages that he can understand and use in daily life. He likes discussions and likes to talk and argue. He may be curious about sex. Clear answers within the Christian framework will keep him maturing.

At eleven, girls may reach 90 percent of their adult height, while boys tend to lag behind one to two years in their growth.

The junior may show his personality by playing the clown or acting silly. He likes the attention this brings. He likes to write plays and maybe even poetry. He is beginning to move into the adult world and may begin to consider his life work. He can think more clearly now, and he enjoys reasoning.

At this age, the camper has few fears and may take unnecessary chances. His humor is slapstick, and he may laugh at another camper's expense. Sometimes guidance is necessary to develop a good, wholesome sense of humor.

He often does not appreciate displays of affection. He will accept a slap on the back or a tug of his ear but no hugs or kisses.

At this age he is usually ready to accept Christ. He knows what sin is—he understands that he is a sinner—and he can know who Christ is and what He has done for him. Most juniors are ready to make a decision in camp if they have not already done so.

The junior is a doer. He is always doing something, and although he may protest, he needs as much as ten hours of sleep.

The junior can become an avid reader. He likes to read about sports, science, airplanes, animals, and outdoor lore, but shuns the make-believe of the primary. He is fascinated by words—big words—and may use them even if he does not know what they mean. He is interested in history and among his peers may become somewhat of an authority on the Civil War or dinosaurs.

His liking to belong to a group provides a basis for organizing the cabin unit. He copies his peers in dress, speech, and mannerisms. He loves pets, including frogs, salamanders, and baby squirrels.

He still has difficulty understanding the symbolism we frequently use when teaching biblical truths.

A junior camper has a good memory. The promise of a hike on Thursday will not be forgotten.

He also has a strong sense of right and wrong. The counselor must not have favorites. Everyone must know the rules before a game begins, or someone will be accused of cheating.

The junior is naturally a hero-worshiper and admires someone of his own sex who is successful in the junior's areas of interest. His heroes change, and the counselor will probably become his hero while he is in camp. He will copy the walk and mannerisms of his hero and watch everything he does.

DEVELOPMENTAL TASKS FOR THE JUNIOR

He needs to take care of his things—put things away.
He needs to assume increasing responsibility for his own conduct.
He needs to learn to respond wholesomely to failure.
He needs to act with integrity in matters of responsibility.
He needs to develop wholesome attitudes toward sex.

He needs to have a relationship with Jesus Christ as Savior and Lord of his life.

He needs to grow in Bible knowledge.

He needs to seek answers to life's problems in the Word.

He needs to develop habits of regular Bible reading and prayer.

He needs to feel personal responsibility for sharing the gospel.

He needs to identify with godly heroes and to pattern his life after them.

He needs to be motivated from within rather than be dependent on outside demands.

THE JUNIOR HIGH CAMPER (ages 12, 13, 14)

CHARACTERISTICS OF THE JUNIOR HIGHER

The junior high age has been called a stress period of life. These campers in the early adolescent period are no longer children but are not yet adults.

The junior high age is a time of growth spurts. A junior higher may grow several inches in a single year. Many of the girls are taller and heavier than boys. There is great variety in stature. The junior high camper often suffers fatigue after periods of extreme energy. Both fellows and girls at this age are frequently awkward and unpoised.

A boy's voice deepens. Girls begin to menstruate. Boys develop sexually. There is a need for self-understanding. Growth is rapid and uneven, appetite is large, the junior higher often is fighting acne, and girls especially want to lose weight. Junior high youth need an alternating quiet and active program and should have nine to ten hours of sleep at this period of rapid and uneven growth.

The junior high camper is able to think abstractly. He is able to see and interpret relationships. He is capable of longer concentration. Attitudes often change, and the eager beaver camper of last year may appear nonchalant and indifferent to everything this year. He tends to make snap judgments without weighing the facts. That he is extremely peer conscious is reflected in dress, attitudes, language, interests, viewpoints, and habits. He appears to know everything, and hesitates to let people know there is anything he does not know.

The junior high camper is very much afraid of being different; he needs group support. A boy may imagine himself a hero or a star basketball player; a girl may imagine herself a beauty queen. Junior highers like adventure and discovery. The scientific method of discovery in outdoor classes can be turned from the revelation in nature to the revelation in the Word. Junior high campers can discover biblical truths for themselves.

The junior high person wants to be grown up; but although he may look like an adult, do not expect adult behavior. A young teen girl may develop a "crush" on her favorite counselor. Junior high campers need limits set for them. This gives a sense of security allowing them to function with freedom within those limits. They want to be independent of adults, yet they still rely heavily on adult guidance and support. Strong loyalties to the peer group develop, yet the junior higher desires times of solitude as well as times with the gang.

Emotionally, he feels misunderstood. He feels no one ever felt as he does right now. All of his emotions are intense—he loves, he hates. He seems to have little control over his emotions, and bursts of anger occur. He needs love, understanding, and security. He is often unpredictable—laughing one minute, crying the next. On Tuesday he will be excited about an overnight camp-out, then decide on Wednesday that he is not interested.

He may doubt God's love for him. If God loves him, he may ask, why did He let his mother die? Or why does God allow wars? He may reevaluate his childhood concepts. He starts to question Scripture—why do we not see miracles today? Doubts arise and basic beliefs break down. He is thinking things through. His religion is becoming *his* personally. He is ready to make an all-out, willing decision for Christ if he has not done so before. He wants to do something for the Lord. He wants to serve Him in school and at home. Often he is ready to dedicate his life to the Lord's work. Without exploiting this youthful idealism, encourage him to commit himself to God's will for his life, whatever or wherever that may be.

Questions such as "What is wrong with _____?" come up in every cabin discussion group. "What should a Christian do about _____?" Questions about dating, drugs, drinking, and sex may be asked. Answers should be given according to biblical principles.

DEVELOPMENTAL TASKS FOR THE JUNIOR HIGHER

He needs to develop a wholesome attitude toward sex from a Christian perspective.
He needs to overcome an attitude of in-group exclusiveness.
He needs to learn to apply himself to a task with sustained attention.
He needs to assume responsibility for his own actions.
He needs to develop control of his emotions.

He needs to direct his affection toward Christ first.

He needs to broaden his friendships beyond a few special friends.

He needs to accept adult assistance when it is required.

He needs to desire God's will for his life.

He needs to be willing to stand for what he knows is right, even if this means standing alone.

He needs to establish a regular habit of Bible reading and prayer.

He needs to experience God speaking to him through the Word.

He needs to become active in a local church.

He needs to become familiar with the basic doctrines in Scripture.

He needs to become aware of the many Christian vocations.

He needs to avoid taking himself too seriously.

He needs to learn how to profit from his mistakes.

He needs to learn how to handle his doubts in the light of Scripture.

He needs to regard his body as the temple of God (1 Cor. 3:16).

THE HIGH SCHOOL CAMPER (AGES 15, 16, 17)

CHARACTERISTICS OF THE HIGH SCHOOLER

Adults are often baffled by teenagers. Teachers, parents, and some camp staff frequently do not feel comfortable with high schoolers. Peer pressures and a desire for popularity may push teens together for protection. Sometimes "going steady" is accepted as a means of not being left out and always having a date. Going steady can mean status.

High schoolers today have a wider circle of friends than did students a generation ago. The automobile has given mobility and enlarged contacts. They are in the midst of cultural change. Community standards of morality are changing. For the Christian teen, there is tension between the biblical standards presented at camp and those of the school, the peer group, and sometimes the home. In today's society, little remains that is clearly accepted as right or wrong. The absolutes of the Bible stand in sharp contrast to the cultural environment teens face.

The camping staff must be honest, and down-to-earth when working with teens. Campers look for consistency. They are searching for answers to life problems, and they have not found satisfying answers in a materialistic and pragmatic society.

Some campers raised in the Sunday school and church have not seen the genuine Christian life demonstrated in many of their Christian contacts. The camp can provide dedicated, vibrant, outgoing, mature friends committed to Jesus Christ.

High schoolers today are physically much more mature than teens a generation ago. They are generally well fed, for we have learned much about nutrition in the past twenty years, but many suffer from a poorly balanced diet. Generally teens are taller, heavier, and healthier than their grandparents were at the same age.

This is an age for experimentation. Senses are keen, and the teenager may try drinking, drugs, and sex. If he has not already experimented in these areas, he is constantly confronted with the temptation in his school. Peer conformity and adult expectations add to his confusion. The teen is looking for a philosophy of life. He needs to see how the pieces of his world fit together.

The high schooler has adult mental capacity, but may not be using his capacity to the full. He knows many things—more than his counselor in some areas. He may have street knowledge that allows him to get along in an urban ghetto. His values may be different from those of the camp staff. He may be disillusioned and cynical, and he may be concerned about his future vocation. The teen may question answers provided at camp. He may not accept adult counsel until the adults have passed his tests of trustworthiness. Many teen ideas come from his peers, even though he can think independently.

The teen is interested in coed activities. Most high schoolers find coed camps more interesting than separate boys' or girls' camps. Both girls and boys are concerned with their appearance and must dress according to the style of their peers. Emotions are still intense among adolescent youth, but they now have better control. The teen likes to live dangerously and will take unnecessary chances. He seeks excitement and thrills.

The teen may be self-conscious because of some physical imperfection. A girl may not like her facial features, acne, or weight. Boys and girls tend to overtax their bodies, and because they feel good they may not eat much except "junk food" and get little sleep. They need eight to nine hours.

Emotional maturity may differ widely. A teen may still be emotionally immature, even though he has grown up in appearance. He may pass a driver's test, yet not be mature enough to drive safely. Some teens have been given almost everything they want, and consequently they do not value highly that which they have. Teens often like the responsibility of leadership, although they may not demonstrate good judgment.

In spiritual areas, the teen may doubt God's love for him because of his past sins. He may question the Bible's accuracy. He sometimes thinks that the Christian life as presented in camp is one of negativism, denying him things he has enjoyed in the past. Or he hesitates to make a decision for Christ because some Christian he has known has failed him or has been inconsistent in the Christian life. Perhaps he has prayed for something and thinks that God did not hear him. He may ask, "How can I know that God is real?" In camp the teen needs opportunity to talk out his problems and understand their roots.

The Christian teen wants to know how to find God's will. He needs to learn how to have a meaningful quiet time and how to study the Bible on his own. He often needs help in knowing which college or Bible school God wants him to attend. He may ask about different Christian vocations.

The camp counselor has a tremendous opportunity for guiding campers as he allows the Holy Spirit through the Word to deal with their needs.

DEVELOPMENTAL TASKS FOR THE HIGH SCHOOLER

He should be able to control his frustrations and emotions.

He should assume responsibility for his actions—not blame someone else.

He should assume responsibility for the consequences of his own decisions.

He should realize that his body is the temple of God and treat it as such.

He should develop the habit of having meaningful personal devotions.

He should learn to postpone immediate pleasures for future goals.

He should be ready to make a meaningful commitment of his life to Jesus Christ.

He should be able to relate biblical principles to everyday life.

He should be aware of the many areas of Christian service open to him.

He should develop good work habits.

He should develop a good self-image.

He should be developing a Christian philosophy of life.

He should act as a responsible Christian and citizen in society.

He should speak up for his Christian convictions and tactfully share them with others.

SUGGESTIONS FOR STUDY

1. Visit a public school classroom of the age level you expect to counsel in camp. What characteristics can you identify? What methods of teaching can you observe in the classroom?
2. For two months teach a Sunday school class of the age group you will have in camp.
3. Take a group of camper age boys and/or girls on an all-day picnic, hike, or camping trip.
4. Offer to work with a Scout troop or club program in your church.
5. Tutor a student in some school subject.
6. In your Sunday school, observe the songs sung in the children's department and list the songs that use symbolism. Which are appropriate for the ages there?
7. Make a list of the characteristics of an age group and beside each one write the implication for camp program.
8. What accounts for the restlessness of primary campers?
9. How can you program in camp to meet the physical needs of primaries?
10. How can you make the Bible study application relevant to your campers' lives?
11. Of what value are rules in camp?
12. How can you program to avoid overfatigue among your junior highers?
13. Keeping in mind total needs, make up a daily schedule for senior highers. Show how each item in your schedule is geared to meet some need.
14. Explain how the imagination of the junior high camper can be helpful in goal setting.
15. Give an example of how you might help a junior higher set his own behavior limits.
16. How would you deal with a camper who doubts that God loves him?
17. How could you counsel a camper who says he has tried Christianity, and it doesn't work?

RESOURCES

Brubaker, J. Omar, and Clark, Robert E. *Understanding People*. Wheaton, Ill.: Evangelical Teacher Training Association, 1972.

Hakes, J. Edward. *An Introduction to Evangelical Christian Education*. Chicago: Moody, 1964.

Ginott, Dr. Haim G. *Between Parent and Child*. New York: Avon, 1969.

Mackay, Joy. *Creative Camping*. Wheaton, Ill.: Victor, 1977.

Moser, Clarence G. *Understanding Boys*. New York: Association 1953.

———. *Understanding Girls*. New York: Association, 1957.

Soderholm, Marjorie E. *Understanding the Pupil*. 3 vols. Grand Rapids: Baker, 1956.

12

Camp Counseling: Working with Campers

J. Omar Brubaker

- *By Personal Example and Attitude*
- *By Leadership*
- *By Using the Small Group*
- *By Applied Guidance*
- *In Dealing with Problems*
- *When Working with Campers*
- *Through Teaching*
- *Through Total Camp Life*

J. OMAR BRUBAKER (M.A., Wheaton College) is associate professor of Christian education, Moody Bible Institute, Chicago, Illinois. He has been active in CCI Midwest Regional since 1968, has worked with Camp Awana (Wisc.), and teaches a camping course at Moody Bible Institute.

Living outdoors with Jesus was an exciting adventure, as his disciples discovered in events such as the seashore experience recorded in John 21. Here, in a typical camp setting, the Master Counselor guided and taught His "camper" group toward the goal of making them more effective disciples.

Camp discipling takes place in the pattern demonstrated by Jesus Christ, the Wonderful Counselor of Isaiah 9. He ministered to the larger group, the crowd. He ministered to individuals, one-to-one. He ministered to the small group, His disciples. He loved them and lived with them. Likewise at camp there is a ministry to the larger unit—a lodge or the whole camp. The key focus, however, is upon the counselor with the individual campers and with the small, or cabin, group.

Camp definitions usually include the concept of the campers' being under guidance, or "under the supervision of trained leadership."[1] The actual process of working with the campers assumes capable leadership on the part of the counselors and other staff members.

Camp may be viewed as three-dimensional. One dimension is the camp itself: the setting, the facilities, the staff—what there is, and what we are at camp. The second is the camp program—what we do. Most important of all, however, is the third or depth dimension—what happens to the camper. Richard S. Doty calls this the character dimension of camping. Achieving depth in camping involves how far the camper moves into the third dimension.[2] The counselor is the key to this dimension of camping.

The high purposes of Christian camping are not accomplished just in Bible classes and devotional times. "Remember that God works all the time, not just after chapel or campfire. Deeper concerns burn in young hearts than many adults realize. As a counselor you will have the privilege of sharing sacred moments if you are alert and sensitive to campers' moods. Maintain an open, approachable spirit throughout the day."[3]

The counselor helps campers by standing *before* them as an example, a leader, a guide, a model; by standing *beside* them as a friend, a companion, a confidant; and by standing *behind* them to

---

1. Floyd Todd and Pauline Todd, *Camping for Christian Youth* (New York: Harper & Row, 1963), p. 29.
2. Richard S. Doty, *The Character Dimension of Camping* (New York: Association, 1960), pp. 24-28.
3. Lloyd D. Mattson, *Camping Guideposts, Handbook for Counselors* (Chicago: Moody, 1972), p. 77.

encourage, prod, and support. He is worth being around. He trusts the Wonderful Counselor and the Holy Spirit to empower, to work through him, and to use him to bring forth fruit in his own life and in the lives of the campers to the glory of God.

Campers are a tremendous responsibility. No wonder the counselor must be at his best. Joy Mackay uniquely summarizes:

They are your responsibility for a week or more. They are looking for a friend. They want a counselor who will help them grow, become independent, and make wise decisions. They want a counselor who will enjoy camp experiences with them. They are looking to see if Christianity works—if it is demonstrated in your life—if what you say agrees with what you are. They want a counselor who is friendly without partiality. They want firmness with love, for this is security. They want to be noticed, to belong, not lost in the shuffle of a large crowd. Your campers want someone to understand them, to listen to them, to give encouragement for a job well done. They watch your every move. Nothing you do will go unnoticed. You are teaching continuously by your attitudes and example.[4]

The Christian camp counselor carries out his counseling ministry through a number of means, ranging from his own personal example to use of the various parts of the camp program. Here are eight means to consider.

BY PERSONAL EXAMPLE AND ATTITUDE

Findley Edge says, "The Christian teacher should seek to embody the ideals of Christ in such an attractive and winsome way that his life will both be worthy of and inspire imitation."[5] The principle *We learn through identification* applied to the counselor means he must be the kind of person the camper will love and respect.

Paul set a high standard by challenging the Corinthians: "Be imitators of me, just as I also am of Christ" (1 Cor. 11:1). Camp staff members should be able to invite campers to do likewise. A good counselor is worth living with, following, talking to, listening to, and imitating. Lloyd D. Mattson says, "Long after games and adventure are forgotten, campers will remember their counselor."[6]

The importance of the counselor's attitude is forcefully described by Joy Mackay:

4. Joy Mackay, *Creative Counseling for Christian Camps* (Wheaton, Ill.: Scripture Press, 1966), p. 21.
5. Finley B. Edge, *Teaching for Results* (Nashville: Broadman, 1956), p. 50.
6. Mattson, p. 21.

Campers pick up your attitudes, your likes and dislikes. They are learning continually. What are they learning from watching you? What are you really teaching them during cleanup time? Have they caught your attitude of "A half-done job is good enough," or have they learned the feeling of self-respect and pride that comes with a job well done? Even washing dirty dishes can be done well to please the Lord!

As you teach the Word of God, do you convey an attitude of "Let's get this over in a hurry so we can go out and have fun"? Or do you approach Bible study with expectancy—"What will God say to us today through His Word?"

Be sure that your reflection of Jesus Christ before your campers is sharp and clear, not blurred by selfish interests or wrong motives. Campers will follow your example. Is it worth copying?[7]

Of course no one feels adequate or is sufficient in himself for this task. Paul asks, "Who is adequate for these things?" He then reminds us that God is. "Not that we are adequate in ourselves to consider anything as coming from ourselves, but our adequacy is from God" (2 Cor. 2:16*b*; 3:5).

By Leadership

What kind of leader is needed in camp? One who helps campers help themselves. He himself has learned and now leads campers in learning. He assesses the situation and involves individuals or the group in thinking through issues and making decisions. He offers suggestions but also a helping hand. He is mature enough not to use people for his own ends.

A. Viola Mitchell, Ida B. Crawford, and Julia D. Robberson list twenty-one characteristics of a good leader in the camping situation:

1. A good leader leads by example. . . .
2. He has a good sense of humor. . . .
3. His thoughts are not inverted toward himself . . . but are extended outward toward the greater "we".
4. In order to tactfully introduce worthwhile ideas or projects, he often capitalizes on the power of suggestion. . . .
5. He tactfully avoids serious misunderstandings and feuds whenever he can, and sincerely attempts to see things from others' viewpoints. . . .
6. When there is work to be done, he is in the midst of it, sleeves rolled up and hands just as dirty as anybody's.

---

7. Mackay, p. 29.

7. He understands the force of group pressure and group opinion. . . .
8. He is ever-mindful of the value of "fun", for happy, self-motivated campers seldom become problems to themselves or others. . . .
9. He knows that campers, no matter how much they complain and grouse, do not really enjoy slovenly, careless standards of conduct or performance. . . .
10. He gives praise freely and can see good in nearly everything and everybody. . . .
11. He foresees an impending crisis and tries to avert it if he can. . . .
12. He shuns public scenes whenever possible. . . .
13. He seldom tells a camper what to do, but discusses the problem with him, skillfully leading him to analyze the situation himself and eventually arrive at his own solution.
14. He never uses physical punishment. . . .
15. He uses disciplinary measures sparingly. . . .
16. He knows that people tend to live up to what others expect of them. . . .
17. He does not take a camper's bad conduct as a personal affront. . . .
18. He satisfies his own basic needs or wishes in a positive way and so keeps himself mentally healthy. . . .
19. He seldom yields to sudden bursts of anger. . . .
20. He is firm but friendly, remaining objective toward all. . . .
21. He takes his position seriously . . . works tirelessly and unceasingly for a cause.[8]

The leader aims to use the democratic process within a biblical framework. He deals with absolutes in biblical content and with certain rules that are fixed and have to be maintained. He does not lead in an authoritarian manner, but with authority. He is not dogmatic, but has convictions. He knows the value of good counsel. "But a wise man is he who listens to counsel" (Prov. 12:15b).

The camp counselor as a leader must be concerned with helping the campers develop abilities relative to leadership and followership. *Camper Guidance, A Basic Handbook for Counselors* suggests the following guidelines:

---

8. A. Viola Mitchell, Julia D. Robberson, and June W. Obley, *Camp Counseling*, 5th ed. (Philadelphia: Saunders, 1977), pp. 143-146.

Leadership may be fostered through:

Knowing and understanding the skills and potentials of your campers.

Helping campers to recognize their own and each other's strengths and weaknesses.

Teaching the group to analyze the purpose of each undertaking before selecting its leader.

Encouraging the group to select its leaders for specific situations for which they are best qualified (i.e., captain of a team, head of a work project, representative to Camper Council.)

Pointing out that leadership requires a willingness to accept responsibility, including the possibility of failure.

Advising the group to select leaders whose motivation is the group need and not simply self-gratification.

Encouraging group participation in varied activities so that a larger number of campers may have the opportunity to qualify for leadership in their own areas of competency.

Looking for and capitalizing on the critical moments for emergence of leaders.

Lending encouragement to new inexperienced leaders.

Being alert to step in and help the leader if he is floundering or going astray.

Followership may be implemented through:

(Followership is defined as: "Ability to serve in a democratic group situation under the leadership of a member of that group but still retain the capacity to suggest, criticize, and evaluate, as well as serve in the project.")

Practicing and stressing the qualities of co-operation, good teamwork, and group effort.

The development of group spirit and loyalty to one's affiliations.

Stressing the importance of each individual's contributions to the success of a project.

Encouraging campers to offer their services where and when needed in the particular skills they can contribute.

Teaching campers to take the initiative and contribute ideas as situations arise. These ideas can sometimes be the most important contribution of all.

Pointing out that effective followership is a most important qualification for eventual leadership.[9]

---

9. Joel W. Bloom et al., *Camper Guidance, A Basic Handbook for Counselors* (Martinsville, Ind.: ACA, 1971), p. 14.

BY USING THE SMALL GROUP

We dare not underestimate the impact of the small group. Mitchell, Robberson, and Obley remind the counselor of this important aspect of camp ministry.

> If you are a cabin counselor, you will be living intimately with your small group nearly twenty-four hours a day, and will come to know them and they to know you very, very well. Remember that decentralized camping came into being to provide just this precise experience of living in a small group, where each member plays an important role and enjoys the feeling of counting as an integral part of his group, sharing in its work, play, joys, and sorrows just as in a close, well-knit family. This is intended to give him a feeling of security and belonging.
>
> Many activities will be within the small group yet, like any well-adjusted family, the group will frequently engage in "community" activities with other groups and the camp as a whole. It will be your job to guide your charges along these desired patterns.[10]

The degree of the counselor's responsibility for the small group will vary in keeping with the camp's philosophy and the program based on it.

A very important dynamic in the camping ministry is how the campers feel about and relate to one another. It is the self-other concept. If a camper feels unwanted, disliked, unaccepted, or threatened, he will not gain very much help from his camping experience. It is likewise of great significance how the campers feel about being at camp—their purpose and resulting motivation.

Not only must the counselor know his individual group members and understand some of these attitudes and feelings, but he must understand how each one can fit into the group and relate properly to one another. A wholesome cabin (group) spirit is essential to achieving camping objectives in the camper. Lloyd D. Mattson suggests, "Helping cabinmates relate warmly to one another creates the spirit that builds a great camp."[11]

Some good questions to ask in connection with cabin life are: How does the camper feel about himself? (A good degree of self-acceptance and healthy, positive self-image are necessary in order to move out to others.) What do the campers expect from each other? What can they contribute to each other in this unique experience together? How can the counselor help them grow through practic-

---

10. Mitchell, Robberson, and Obley, pp. 87-88.
11. Mattson, p. 22.

ing the biblical principles of treating others as you want to be treated and loving your neighbor as yourself?

Group living contributes to achieving goals such as:

Deciding ways of behavior
Developing a deeper sense of security
Understanding and accepting others
Learning to fit in
Experiencing the feeling of respect and acceptance by others
Enjoying the freedom and pleasure of living in a self-sustaining
    group
Respecting the rights of others   .
Accepting certain responsibilities.

These social objectives are achieved only with the warm support of fellow campers under the guidance of a socially and emotionally mature counselor. The leader should encourage a permissive group atmosphere to the extent that campers can feel free to voice what they are really thinking and feeling. They need to share what concerns them and where they hurt. Then they should experience from other Christian campers what should be true in the body of Christ: "That the members should have the same care for one another" (1 Cor. 12:25b).

By Applied Guidance

In carrying out his ministry, the counselor is beside the camper as friend, confidant, and companion; he loves, listens, cares, asks, shares, and guides.

In Loving and Caring

Under the Spirit's control, the counselor is the channel of God's love. This is possible "because the love of God has been poured out within our hearts through the Holy Spirit who was given to us" (Rom. 5:5b). The personal concern is so important in camping. Lynn and Campbell Loughmiller note, "Few things can be more important in camping than the over-all spirit of friendliness growing out of an interest in, and concern for, each individual." Regarding how campers feel, these authors write, "They are quick to size up a counselor as a person who really likes them or as one who is simply 'doing his duty.' This over-all, inclusive interest in each camper constitutes a spiritual environment most conducive to growth."[12]

AS A LISTENER

The counselor demonstrates personal concern by taking time and being available. He is patient and sensitive. He talks and listens at the camper's level, has a positive attitude, and is shockproof. How well do I listen? is a good question. Jesus said, "Therefore take care how you listen" (Luke 8:18). This not only relates to learning but also applies to teaching and counseling.

ASKING QUESTIONS

The counselor asks questions to gain information. Questions help to clarify comments and issues. The counselor's question can cause a camper to think more deeply. In the process of counseling, questions help to probe, challenge, and confront.

BY PERSONAL SHARING

An appropriate comment can cause reflection, provide sympathetic support, and show empathy. Sharing from life and experience, the counselor shows he understands and may provide reinforcement.

The counselor effectively works with a camper in a counseling situation when he listens, reflects, clarifies, and guides the camper in finding solutions and taking action. "Personal counseling aims at helping campers discover their problems and voluntarily apply a solution."[13] The Christian counselor should be especially adept in using the Word of God so that the camper can find God's truth relevant to his situation and need. It will be more meaningful to the camper if he is guided to see the truth for himself.

IN DEALING WITH PROBLEMS

How the counselor deals with problems can help the camper grow. The counselor can first of all share out of experience how he has dealt with his own problems, since he is not without them. Realistically sharing out of success and failure, the counselor can let

---

12. Lynn Loughmiller and Campbell Loughmiller, *Camping and Christian Growth* (New York: Abingdon-Cokesbury, 1953), pp. 36-37.
13. Mattson, p. 109.

it be known that he is made of the same stuff as is the camper. Thus the camper can more easily identify with him. This is one great value of Christ's having lived as we live. "For we do not have a high priest who cannot sympathize with our weaknesses, but one who has been tempted in all things as we are, yet without sin" (Heb. 4:15).

As a counselor helps a camper solve his problems and grow, he can introduce principles of leadership and Christian maturity so that the camper not only helps himself but also begins to share with others and help them.

Helping someone solve problems involves getting beneath the surface to get at the root causes and not just the symptoms. You help the camper gain insight that will enable him to arrive at a solution. You help the individual take responsibility for his problem. Problem solving from a Christ-centered, Bible-based perspective will help the camper have a relationship to the Lord as his helper. He can learn to depend upon His help and to use the Word of God for himself. Prayer becomes meaningful as the camper learns to commit his situation to the Lord and trust Him to work in his behalf.

Campers come equipped with small problems and large ones. These may be individual needs, or they may involve the group. Misbehavior stems from a variety of causes. Joel W. Bloom lists some questions that help determine causes of misbehavior, and he gives recommendations for dealing with such problems.

Things to consider when a camper misbehaves:

Are poor relationships with campers and counselors a factor?
Are you the right counselor for this camper?
Do you think the camper is in the right group?
Is the group atmosphere or climate a factor in the camper's misbehavior?
Is the camper getting sufficient success and satisfaction from the camping experience?
Does the camper appear to have any serious worries, anxieties, or fears that might be causative or limiting factors?
Could poor health be a factor in the camper's behavior?

Some general recommendations for dealing with misbehavior:

Try to establish and maintain an understanding relationship with the camper.
Recognize that there are usually specific reasons why a child misbehaves. Try to find out what his reasons are.

Try to provide more wholesome means for the camper to fulfill the
need he was trying to satisfy.
If others in the group are affected, let them know the situation is
being handled and their rights protected.
Approach the camper with kindly firmness and use discipline and
controls with a sense of justice.
Be sure to conform to the basic principles of discipline and control:
consistency, suitability and flexibility.
Make sure that discipline and controls are meaningful and in keeping
with the misbehavior.[14]

The counselor cannot solve his camper's problems for him but
should guide him into the Word of God where the Holy Spirit can
speak to him and where he can find principles for making right
choices. Joy Mackay offers this good reminder: "Your campers cannot take you home with them after camp, to solve their problems all
through the year. But they can take along Christ, who has promised
never to leave or forsake His own (Heb. 13:5)."[15]

WHEN WORKING WITH CAMPERS

Opportunities abound for a counselor to be with and help his
campers. A helping hand or a word of encouragement may be given
in the craft shop or in the nature center. The opportunity may come
in connection with cabin chores or other assigned tasks. Often a
counselor can help with a camper's learning or improving in a skills
area such as archery, swimming, canoeing, or horsemanship. Or
help could be given in sports or game playing. Though the counselor
may not be the teacher or leader in these areas, he can often be with
his campers in a support role.

If campers are to help with various work assignments around the
camp, the counselor is the key to helping them make the most of
such responsibilities.

Working together should help teach the appreciation and dignity of
work and should be an enjoyable time of joking and singing, as well as
contribute as a group to camp living. Work should never be doled out
as punishment. Your own attitude toward work is important, for if you
make a game of it, an enjoyable time will be had by all. Though your
supervision may not be needed on chores, this should be a time of
enjoying your campers' company and they yours. It should not be
"I'm here to see that you do the job right," but, "Let's do this job
quickly together."

14. Bloom et al., p. 15.
15. Mackay, pp. 30-31.

Work can be a fulfillment of a camper's needs. Even grubby, menial tasks can help fulfill one's self-esteem and boost his security. Work can be made joyous and creative.[16]

THROUGH TEACHING

Teaching is accomplished by guidance, not simply by lecturing or telling. Teaching in camp should be concerned with "eaching," that is, showing concern and interest to each camper in light of his needs and interests. The counselor may be guiding one camper in his Bible study or leading the group in a discussion during rest hour or cabin devotions, but he can be teaching very effectively.

In the book of Acts, the Lord told Philip, "Go up and join [literally, "glue yourself to"] this chariot." Finding the Ethiopian eunuch reading Isaiah the prophet, Philip asked, "Do you understand what you are reading?" The man's question in response is a good reminder of the counselor's responsibility in his teaching role. "Well, how could I, unless someone guides me?" (Acts 8:29-31). In many settings at camp, whether formal (a Bible class or camp vesper service) or informal (a cabin devotional or casual conversation), the counselor can communicate spiritual truth effectively as he shares out of his experience in the Word, guided by the Holy Spirit, in relation to the need at hand.

Counselors teach in various ways. They can teach without words that it is important to follow the camp's "clean grounds" rules. Let the counselor drop litter on the ground, and the campers will follow. If he picks up along the way, so will they. When he stands at attention during the flag-raising ceremony, they will learn by his example. Likewise, when counselors complain about the food, use unkind words, or make critical comments, campers will do the same.

THROUGH TOTAL CAMP LIFE

Throughout the camp period the campers will be learning.[17] Since first impressions are most important, everything and everyone should be in readiness when the campers arrive. The counselor will be largely responsible to make them feel.welcome, to introduce them to others, and to provide a sense of security by helping them get settled in their living area. A key objective is furthering group unity and feelings of acceptance from the beginning.

---

16. Ibid., pp. 14-15.
17. Joel W. Bloom, *Camper Guidance in the Routines of Daily Living* (Martinsville, Ind.: ACA, 1965), pp. 2-11.

Since a major camp objective is to teach the campers self-reliance, they can be encouraged to do things for themselves as well as to help others. At camp they can learn to spend time profitably and to entertain themselves as well as find enjoyment with others. They acquire new skills, especially those related to the out-of-doors.

In areas of personal hygiene, many campers can learn better ways to care for themselves. Through proper health care and safety measures they can learn to appreciate the wonder of their bodies. This is probably the greatest area of concern of parents for their children. The psalmist said, "I will give thanks to Thee, for I am fearfully and wonderfully made; wonderful are Thy works, and my soul knows it very well" (Psalm 139:14).

Many things can be learned in the camp dining hall. Orderly procedures need to be followed in coming to meals and leaving afterward. Some spiritual lessons can be learned in the areas of praise and thanksgiving. Accepting God's good gifts of food with thanksgiving eliminates pickiness and waste at mealtime. The atmosphere should be one of relaxation with peace and quiet, while providing opportunity for friendly conversation and fun. The counselor's example in attitude, conduct, conversation, and eating habits is of extreme significance. Campers can learn to improve table manners, be more thankful and gracious, and eat some things they may have been fussy about. They also need to know the value of a balanced diet.

Rest is refreshing, and sleep is necessary at camp. Rest hour usually comes after lunch and helps rejuvenate campers for the remainder of the day. Campers can learn during the quiet activities usually permitted at this time. Since camp life is strenuous and busy, proper rest and plenty of sleep at night are necessary to enjoy it to the full. Campers should leave camp rested and healthy instead of being completely exhausted.

A major function of the counselor is to help the camper be actively involved in the camp program each day. The more decentralized the program, the greater will be the counselor's responsibility. When are the goals of camping being accomplished in the lives of campers? When are they learning and growing? Camp provides a wide variety of effective settings:

1. In the small group, the cabin group—during cabin devotions, clean up, rest hour, free time, camp-outs
2. Alone, individually—personal devotions, free time, personal care and hygiene, preparation for classes, Bible reading, study
3. Together with a friend or a few friends

4. Alone with the counselor or another staff member—individual instruction, counseling
5. In small-group activity in the camp program—work groups, Bible class, nature and craft activities, music, dramatics, sports teams, skills classes, and other recreation groups
6. In the larger group—the dining hall, chapel, vespers, around the campfire, other all-camp or large-group activities.

Campers learn through class instruction, by living together and working together, by playing and serving—so many ways. They learn in the cabin, in a tent, by the lake, in the chapel, around the campfire, along the trail, lying in bed, around the table—so many places.

In their busy days at camp, campers learn best by doing those things that result in the development of skills, personal achievement, and growth—swimming, sailing, archery, tripping, campcraft skills, nature study and woodsmanship, canoeing.

Campers like to anticipate new and exciting experiences. They enjoy remembering good times. They want to repeat satisfying activities. The counselor plays a large part in careful planning with them to see that their activities are worthwhile and rewarding.

At camp, principles of Christian living are demonstrated, related, and practiced in everyday living, not just taught in chapel or discussed in Bible class. One camper said, "Back in church and Sunday school they teach us the Bible, but here they expect us to live it!" What is read in the Bible during private devotions or discussed in cabin devotions must be "tried on for size." To be really learned, truth must be lived. Camp is a laboratory for Christian living, a proving ground where spiritual truths are tested and practiced during camp's many activities.

A camper's radar is always on! What attitudes are learned from the camp staff? How much will the campers grow? The counselor's love and loyalty to God and His Word, appreciation of the works of the Lord in nature, skill in working with campers, openness to the control of the Holy Spirit, dedication to the camper and his task, relationships with other staff members, and love for the campers will help determine the answer in the providence of God.

SUGGESTIONS FOR STUDY

1. How does the example of Jesus' ministry help the counselor in working with campers?
2. What are the implications of the third dimension of camping for Christian camps?
3. According to this chapter, in what ways does the counselor help the camper grow?
4. What is the camp counselor's role as a leader?
5. How can he foster leadership in the lives of the campers?
6. What are some guidelines for dealing with camper problems?
7. How does the camp counselor serve as a teacher?
8. What tips relating to camper guidance would you give a new counselor?
9. Survey some camp counselors. Ask for guidelines and illustrations from their experience relating to the various ways a counselor helps campers.
10. Develop a counselor's job description based on information in this chapter.
11. Survey some campers and ask how their camp counselor helped them in the major areas covered in this chapter.

RESOURCES

Doty, Richard S. *The Character Dimension of Camping.* New York: Association, 1960.
How to Be a Camp Counselor. Wheaton, Ill.: Scripture Press, 1967.
Mackay, Joy. *Creative Camping.* Wheaton, Ill.: Victor, 1977.
Mattson, Lloyd D. *Camping Guideposts.* Chicago: Moody, 1972.
——— *Foul-up or Follow-up?* Wheaton, Ill.: Victor, 1974.
——— *Way to Grow.* Wheaton, Ill.: Victor, 1973.
Mitchell, A. Viola; Robberson, Julia D.; and Obley, June W. *Camp Counseling.* 5th ed. Philadelphia: Saunders, 1977.
Todd, Floyd, and Todd, Pauline. *Camping for Christian Youth.* New York: Harper & Row, 1963.
Wright, H. Norman. *Help! I'm a Camp Counselor.* Glendale, Calif.: Regal, 1968.

Unit 4

Christian Camp Management

This unit deals with what might be termed the business aspects of camping. There are bills to be paid, reports to be filed, buildings to be built, and manpower to be developed.

Following its ofttimes informal, easy-going development, Christian camping today has before it the challenge of continuing growth in professional management and operational procedures. This unit on camp administration seeks to encourage high standards—growth toward excellence.

The first chapter looks at basic *organizational patterns* of sponsorship and management direction. It also includes a section on management issues, which those concerned with the future of camping must seriously consider.

A second chapter discusses the crucial area of *camp facilities*. A campsite consultant projects the why and what of site rental compared with site purchase, as well as the planning that goes into effective use of buildings and property.

The future of Christian camping is directly linked to the quality of its leadership. The director of a college-level camping degree program reviews camping as a profession and the *professional training* involved.

As the executive director of Christian Camping International has pointed out, Christian camps need to set their sights on quality. It is in this vein that authors Lloyd D. Mattson, Clifford V. Anderson, C. June Stump, and Bill V. Bynum write about the practical professional aspects of Christian camping.

13

Sponsorship and Organization

Lloyd D. Mattson

- *Camp Sponsorship*
- *Camp Management*
- *Camping Issues*

Informal camping has little problem with management details. However, in the organized camping we are considering in this book, good administration is essential. While the spiritual values in Christian camping remain a primary factor, from the aspect of sound, productive business procedures and also the increasing pressure of regulatory standards, good camp management is vital.

This chapter considers the various types of sponsorship involved in Christian camping. It discusses management especially as related to the board of directors and the position of executive director.

The chapter also contains a section dealing with current issues of concern to those responsible for camp direction.

CAMP SPONSORSHIP

Camping today is sponsored by a wide range of organizations or organizational groups. Many of these own their own campsites, although such ownership is rapidly becoming more difficult. The alternative is facility rental or joint ownership.

Most Christian camping programs are extensions of broader ministries such as a local church, a denomination, or a mission agency. Thus the person interested in camping involvement will find contacts in many levels of Christian ministry.

DENOMINATIONAL CAMPS

Many of the camp meetings and early Bible conferences grew out of the concern of denominational leaders to extend their movements through the evident strength of an extended meeting in the controlled environment of the assembly away from home. Some of today's strong youth camps trace their roots to those early, adult-oriented conferences.

Youth camps and retreat centers are operated today by most denominations; these are usually on a regional or district level. The sixties and seventies witnessed an upsurge of interest in family camps, retreats, and special interest programs for youth and adults. Camping has also become a year-round ministry, and it is not uncommon for denominational camps to report more camper days during the fall, winter, and spring than for the summer.

Denominational camps, drawing heavily on volunteers, call on pastors and lay persons to fill staff positions. While adequate training for these volunteers has sometimes been lacking, camping owes a great deal to the pioneering efforts of denominational camping leaders. Likewise, denominations owe much to the camping ministry, as evidenced by the camp commitments recorded in missionary biographies and pastors' profiles.

THE INTER-CHURCH CAMP

Some camps, usually with smaller facilities and operating only for the summer season, are sponsored by a group of area churches.

Independent churches and those distant from their denominational camps benefit from this cooperative association.

Quite often such camps struggle for funds and staff. A camp may be the vision and burden of one person or a small group of persons. Increasing government regulations and the growing demand for higher standards threaten many of these camps.

THE INDIVIDUAL CHURCH CAMP

The church-owned camp offers many advantages for lay leadership. However, the cost of maintenance and the demands on church staff members must be weighed against these advantages. Many larger churches have concluded that it is more practical to rent than to own a camp facility.

THE MISSION AGENCY CAMP

Just as general camping was strengthened by the innovations of the agency camps of YMCA and Scouting, so Christian camping has benefited from program concepts developed by mission agency camps.

Christian Service Brigade, Pioneer Girls, Awana Clubs, Bible Memory Association, Child Evangelism, Young Life, Inter-Varsity, and similar mission movements have included camping in their ministries. Lacking the sometimes inhibiting force of long tradition, these agencies have been free to break new ground in camp philosophy and program.

The Christian agency camp often recruited leaders with training and experience in general agency camps. These introduced proved methods for serving youth in the outdoors. Camp programs were enhanced by the achievement emphasis and other program distinctives within the agency.

THE SCHOOL-SPONSORED CAMP

Though relatively few in number, school-sponsored camps have contributed greatly to advances made in the Christian camping movement.

Camp Honey Rock, sponsored by Wheaton College, is perhaps the best known of the school camps. Described as the college's Northwoods Campus, Honey Rock has served as a training center and laboratory camp for many hundreds of college students.

A practical expression of Christian school influence in camping is seen in the growing number of school-affiliated training programs being conducted in camps. Increasingly, college and Bible school deans are recognizing the credit validity of camp-related academic studies and field experience.

THE INDEPENDENT CHRISTIAN CAMP

Some of the most progressive camp and conference ministries to be found have grown out of the vision of an individual or a group of persons who have founded independent camping centers.

Lacking the loyalty of an established constituency, the independent camp must build its following through the appeal of its program and facilities. Often this has led to innovative programming for campers and staff that has set the pace in camping development.

Independent camp leaders were prominent in the founding of Christian Camping International. Facilities provided by independent camps are widely used today by churches, denominations, and Christian agencies who choose not to develop their own campsites.

Independent camps range from relatively small facilities serving only youth to large multipurpose conference centers that sometimes include several campsites designed for various age levels.

Prominent independent camp centers include Word of Life and Camp of the Woods (New York); Forest Home, Hume Lake, and Mt. Hermon (California); and Maranatha (Michigan).

THE WILDERNESS/TRAVEL CAMP

While trail camping has been a part of some Christian camps for many years, only since the sixties have distinctive wilderness programs and travel camps come into prominence.

Wilderness/travel camps include traditional canoe and backpack trips, bicycle treks, and tours. While many camps of this nature are program features of resident camps or conferences, organizations specializing in the wilderness/travel activity are growing in number.

CAMP MANAGEMENT

The student of camping will become aware that efficient administration has sometimes been lacking on the camping scene. This can be related somewhat to the early history of camping when camp was but a small part of the total responsibility of church and denominational programs.

As the camping movement grew, larger camp centers found it

necessary to recruit professional leadership and to adopt effective management procedures. Today camp administration is becoming somewhat standardized, although a wide variety of organizational patterns will be noted.

Most camps operate under the direction of a board of directors who manage the camp for a denomination, agency, or constituency. The independent camp, of course, establishes its own board, usually self-perpetuating and guided by the philosophy and objectives contained in constitution and bylaws.

The management of a camp or conference is guided by the nature of its ministry. An executive officer, usually known as the director, supervises persons responsible for business affairs, property, program, health, food service, counseling staff, and perhaps promotion and public relations. Obviously, a smaller camp will require fewer staff members and each one often receives several assignments. The need for a carefully planned management strategy is underscored by the multiple facets of the camp operation.

Licensing of camps is expected to eventually become the rule, and standards will be imposed on all camps, large and small. Management will be compelled to upgrade buildings, bring kitchens and sanitary facilities up to safe standards, and strengthen the camp staff.

THE CAMP BOARD

The camp board is responsible to oversee the total camp operation in the interest of the sponsoring agency. Board members are usually elected or appointed by the agency or, in the case of independent camps, recruited from a group of interested persons.

The board is responsible to set policy and approve budgets and becomes the legal entity that enters into contracts and holds property. The executive director of the camp reports to the board and implements the board's policies and directives.

Camps that are relatively small may operate without permanent staff. The camp board then assumes the duties of executive director by recruiting seasonal personnel and supervising operations. This obviously lacks efficiency and often results in a weak program.

Few jobs demand so many skills as those required of the director of a Christian camp. The aggressive support of the camp board is vital to the director and to the camp's effective ministry.

THE EXECUTIVE DIRECTOR

As a camp grows beyond the one-man-staff status, an executive director must be secured. This person often has little direct involvement with program operations but must concern himself with business and supervision of staff.

The executive director's immediate staff should include clerical persons and personnel to manage accounting and business. The number of persons in administrative work will depend on the size of the camp. Promotion and public relations, fund raising, attending to government reports and insurance matters, and managing large budgets are all duties of the executive director.

CAMPING ISSUES

Camp management must deal with many aspects of the camping enterprise. Without considering each in depth, the following list notes some of the major issues involved in camp direction.†

PROPERTY

Securing and maintaining the camp property has become one of the major items on camp management's agenda. Thoughts of exploding land costs, mounting pressures to tax camp lands, the encroachment of urban sprawl or private development incompatible with the camp atmosphere, and the inevitable program limitations imposed by a given campsite will occupy the minds of the executive director and the camp board.

Can the property serve both day campers and resident campers? Does a secluded area exist where outpost camping can be offered? What about the use of horses on the camp property? Will local zoning permit hookups for recreational vehicles? What problems lie ahead should it be desirable to expand the sewer system? Many property-related issues must be faced as management plans for the future.

STANDARDS

The national camping organizations will continue to set guidelines for the operation of camps. This is essential for upgrading the average camp, although some individual camps are far ahead of others in their search for excellence. Some leaders are concerned over the growing prospect of government regulation of camp operation. Some are opposed to the expenditures that will be generated by

†This section prepared by Clifford V. Anderson.

new laws. Others are in principle opposed to government interference. Some are concerned over religious freedom. National involvement is proposed because state legislation varies greatly, and minimum regulations insuring health and safety of campers are required for protecting children at camp. Present proposed legislation protects the rights of camps and their sponsoring groups to conduct religious programs.[1] American Camping Association and Christian Camping International keep their members informed of developments and examine member camps for accrediting purposes.

COSTS

Financing camps will be a continuing challenge. Operating on a "shoestring" will not be possible except for wilderness trail camps where campers provide their own labor, and where property costs are minimal. However, leadership and equipment costs still exist in the trail-type camp. Donation of materials and labor have kept costs down, but camp boards and directors will need ingenuity to operate successful camps that can compete in the market. Supporters of camping will need to be recruited so that camp fees do not become prohibitive to most families. Scholarships for needy children should be available lest camping become a middle- and upper-class activity only.

NUMBERS

The development of the recreational vehicle and related equipment has contributed to the growth of family camping. This has cut into the enrollment at private and organizational camps. When families budget for a vacation via camping they may have less sense of need for peer-related camping for their children. The growing school-camp movement will have the effect of both familiarizing more students with camping out and meeting the need for such in some families. Its effect is difficult to assess, although the school camp makes it possible for camps to use their property in the so-called off-season, thus providing income for the camp ministry.

Population trends need not overly concern camps since only a relative minority of children of school age attend. Overall, there will be some increase of elementary school children in the future because of the number of women coming to the child-bearing age, even though families will be smaller in size.

1. John W. Baker, "Safety Bills No Threat to Liberty," *Report From the Capital*, November 1975, pp. 5, 7.

VOLUNTEER STAFF

Some church-related camps have used volunteer counselor, program, and operations staff for many years. This is how cost per camper has been kept low. Serious questions are raised, however, when volunteers are unable to effectively contribute to the mission of the camp. When a staff is volunteer, training and supervision are sometimes difficult. When volunteers *can* be found, trained, and guided in their ministry so that the mission of the camp is realized, then much can be said for their use.

BUSINESS OR MINISTRY?

Institutional maintenance, while necessary, can so dominate concern that mission is jeopardized. Camps, like churches, are not immune to this pressure to devote time, energy, and financial resources to the building of an institution while giving limited attention to its primary task. Of course, without careful business procedures camps will be "out of business" and unable to serve, but mission must take precedence over maintenance.

PHILOSOPHY

Camps start with a purpose and come to have a method of operation that is often hammered out with experience. Changes come. Are they thought out and accepted because they are a logical outgrowth of our philosophy of education? Are we aware of the tremendous potential that is present in a twenty-four-hour-a-day involvement in the lives of campers? Do we understand how learning occurs and the methods that facilitate it? Whom are we set up to serve, and why? What do we want to happen through camping in our setting? These and other questions provide food for thought on program, staffing, daily schedule, promotion, and the entire operation of a camp.

CREATIVITY

Hedley G. Dimock, son of H. S. Dimock, researcher and teacher of a generation of camp leaders, has written:

> Time was when camping led the educational movement with its flexible, experimental, child-centered approach; when it made an excellent reputation for itself as the way to spend a worthwhile summer. Not so, today, as school teaching has taken the lead with activist

educational methods, ungraded schools, and working to level programs. Camps have become institutionalized around their former successes and are resistant to change. They are content to rest on the laurels of the past . . . . I am gravely concerned that residential camping is being phased out of playing a significant role in the education and development of youth.[2]

It is easy to become imprisoned by our past success. Through meetings and journals the professional must help leadership stay fresh. Suggestions and criticism from parents, campers, and staff should be encouraged and heard. We must be open and ready to make productive changes in programming, staffing, and decision making.

COOPERATION WITH THE CHURCH

Camping has long had a close relationship to institutions that purpose to serve mankind and build individual character. The church, however, is not just an ally to camp, but Christian camps exist as part of the church's mission. In the busy enterprise of education, recreation, and religion at camps and conference grounds, it is possible to ignore the church. Independent camps and conference grounds do well to remember their purpose and build sound relationships with the churches of the area.

The church of the Lord Jesus Christ is more important than its agencies, although they are cooperating ministries helping it fulfill its mission. More effort at follow-up of campers and more equipping the laity to minister at home will bring rich dividends to both church and camp.

---

2. Hedley G. Dimock, "Camping's Resistance to Change," *The Camping Magazine*, February 1968, pp. 19-20.

SUGGESTIONS FOR STUDY

1. Identify the seven basic kinds of camp sponsorship described in the chapter and give an example of at least five kinds, listing several key objectives for each example.
2. Discuss the values of the school-related camp to the educational goals of the school.
3. Prepare a report on the values of camping to a Christian missionary agency (Christian Service Brigade, Pioneer Girls, Campus Life, or a similar organization).
4. Construct an organizational chart for a camp with which you are familiar.
5. Describe the basic functions of a camp board.
6. List the primary duties of a camp executive director.
7. In what ways do government agencies influence the direction of Christian camp development?
8. Report on the standards and accrediting programs of the American Camping Association or Christian Camping International (addresses in Appendix).
9. Write a brief paper on the relationships between the Christian camp and the local church.
10. Report on a current news article that relates to one of the camping issues listed in the chapter.

RESOURCES

Dimock, Hedley S. *Administration of the Modern Camp.* New York: Association, 1957.
Ford, Phyllis M., and Rodney, Lynn S. *Camp Administration.* New York: Wiley, 1973.
Ledlie, John, ed. *Managing the YMCA Camp.* New York: Association, 1961.

Also note the materials listed under the resource section in chapter 14.

14

Camp Facilities

C. June Stump

- *The Campsite*
- *Camp Facilities*
- *Maintaining Site and Facilities*

It has been estimated that more than six thousand campsites dedicated to Christian ministries are currently operating in the United States and Canada. The commercial value of these campsites would exceed $1.5 billion, with annual operating costs running well

C. JUNE STUMP (B.A., Moody Bible Institute) has been a Christian campsite consultant since 1967. She has directed Pioneer Girls camps and has been active in ACA.

199

over $100 million. Certainly in the area of facilities, Christian camping is big business.

The importance of careful site and facility planning seems obvious, yet the nature of Christian camping's development has sometimes led camp sponsors to approach planning in a haphazard manner. This chapter will discuss the rationale for and approach to professional planning for site and facility development.

While the discussion may at times become technical, it is vital for the student of camping to understand the essential relationship between Christian camping and its physical properties. Very often the persons responsible for developing the property have had minimal knowledge of sound camping philosophy. As a result, land use and buildings have been ill fitted to the purposes of program planners and the needs of campers.

The role of the professional camp consultant and architect will be pointed out. Whether a new site is being considered, or major changes planned in an established site, professional help should be sought simply by way of good stewardship. The cost involved will be recovered through escaping the costly errors that usually follow when unprepared leadership attempts major developments without guidance.

The Campsite

Campsites may be owned by the camp, or rented. Some consist of hundreds of acres, others are quite small. Even trip and travel camps require a place to meet and plan, or to develop basic skills before the trip, as well as a place to debrief when it is over. Seldom is a site ideal, and the site that is excellent for one camp program may not adequately meet the needs of another. How can we evaluate? What must be considered?

SITE AND PROGRAM

Just as philosophy determines program, so *program determines site*. The most important criterion for site selection or evaluation is that the site meet the requirements of the anticipated camping program. Obviously, a wilderness camping program needs wilderness; a small craft program requires a suitable body of open water.

The very word *camping* suggests living in the natural environment. This has implications for the camp's site. While you can rappel down the bank of a gravel pit, how much more satisfying it is to rappel down the side of a mountain, where everything around you is congruous with the experience.

Yet, to some extent *site determines program*. Perhaps your new site has natural features that will enable you to add unanticipated new dimensions to your program. For example, a variety of rocks are found on the site—encouraging interest in geology. Or, you discover a marsh community with unique nature program potential. It is possible that excellent program potential is overlooked even on sites that have been used for many years.

Sometimes a site problem modifies program. One director found her new camp's waterfront unsuitable for swimming, and further investigation indicated the situation could not be corrected. Swimming was an important part of the camp's program. The first year, the campers had to hike a half mile or so to a public beach. Then the camp made arrangements to use a private beach across the lake, bought a pontoon boat, and ferried campers back and forth. The daily schedule had to be modified to fit the situation, but a site limitation was turned into an added experience for campers.

SELECTING A DEVELOPED SITE TO RENT

For camps with limited campers and camping weeks it is feasible to look for a campsite to rent before attempting any land purchase.

Some state and national parks have resident campsites available at nominal cost. The directories listing member camps of Christian Camping International and the American Camping Association will be helpful in searching for rental facilities. Contact the camps in your area to see if time is available. Then visit a promising site and evaluate its suitability for your program, following the basic guidelines found on page 202.

Special problems are associated with renting. Renters often get the least desirable choice of weeks. The site and facilities may be inadequate for your type of program. Renting may require the moving and storing of equipment during the off season. As your camp program expands, and more weeks are needed, rental sites may become more difficult to find. At this point, of course, it might be appropriate to begin searching for property.

SELECTING A SITE TO PURCHASE

Responsible board. Before starting the search for property, a non-profit organization should be formed in the state where the group expects to buy. The board representing this organization will need to be concerned with the following areas: law, finance, promotion, public relations, camp operation, site selection, and eventually site development and maintenance. For committee work some of these may be combined.

The biggest question probably will be, Where will the money come from? Securing and developing a site requires considerable capital expenditure that cannot possibly be secured from camper fees. A broad fund-raising plan needs to be developed, often with the help of fund-raising specialists.

Constituency support. Generating enthusiasm for the project is important. This can be done by keeping the constituency informed, enlisting prayer support, and building confidence in the board's leadership. The broader the financial base, the stronger the camp's position.

Securing a federal nonprofit corporation tax-exempt status allows the camp to issue tax-exempt receipts for gifts. In some states, a state sales tax exemption may also be secured.

Some camps find it possible to issue low interest notes or bonds. In a few cases, a selective cut of property timber may be helpful in defraying development costs. This should be undertaken only after careful study of long-range needs and after consultation with state forestry officials.

Know what you are looking for in a campsite. Some specific questions you need to answer are:
1. What type of programs are being planned—for example, family camping, day camping, camps for senior citizens or the handicapped, outdoor education, retreats? Is an area needed for picnics or for recreational vehicles?
2. What will be the maximum number of campers per week?
3. How will campers be organized? Large groups or small living units?
4. Where is your supporting constituency located?
5. What degree of willingness to support a camp can be anticipated?
6. Where are attractive areas for locating a camp? Travel time for the constituency?
7. Will camp ownership really supplement the program of the local churches? How?
8. What will be the camp's unique contribution?

Basic guidelines for a site.
1. Acreage—ideally one acre of land per camper, either owned by camp or available for its use on adjacent public lands. This stan-

dard is generally accepted in the United States to prevent over-use of the camp environment.

2. Terrain—ideally more wooded than cleared land; gently rolling rather than flat. Free from natural hazards.

3. Privacy—a minimum of public road frontage, and none dividing the property. Secluded, with a buffer from neighbors.

4. Soil—good drainage is an asset. Sandy soils are excellent; clay poor. However, very sandy soil can be unstable and subject to erosion.

5. Accessibility—maximum two to four hours travel time for most of the constituency is considered good. An all-weather road approach is necessary for year-round use.

6. Natural beauty—appealing as a campsite, having a variety of trees, shrubs, wild flowers, and wildlife.

7. Safety—ideally within thirty minutes from doctor, hospital, and fire protection.

8. Utilities—adequate drinking water, electricity, and phone available at reasonable cost.

9. Open water—suitable for swimming and small craft, adequate for the camp capacity anticipated. Sometimes this can be developed on the property.

Evaluation of a proposed site. The site search committee should look at as many properties as possible. If promising property is located, hike the property—in various kinds of weather, if possible—checking carefully against the basic guidelines. If it still looks good, it is wise to call in a camp consultant for a feasibility study. Ideally, the same person will guide you throughout the development of your property, should the decision to purchase be made.

Further investigations of the property with the consultant. (The property could be held with earnest money or a binder.)

A camp consultant will be concerned with a survey of soils and a more in-depth study of the site, including any existing structures. It is very important that you thoroughly acquaint the camp consultant with your particular camp program requirements in order for the feasibility of this property *for your use* to be correctly evaluated.

Other questions to be considered are: Are there any easements on the property? Are mineral or water rights available? Is the title clear?

TAKING OVER A DEVELOPED CAMP

Perhaps a camp has "inherited" a site that is already developed. It may have been used for a number of years. Although the campsite may be basically functional, professional help is advised should any of the following apply.

1. You need to expand your summer capacity and require new facilities.
2. You want to make a change in some, or all, of the living units.
3. Serious problems with the existing sanitation system need to be solved.
4. Additional land purchase is being considered or has been made.
5. A major building, such as the dining hall, is inadequate.
6. More off-season use of the site is desired.
7. It is felt that camp is not utilizing its property as wisely as it could.
8. There is no current long-range site plan.

Other problems to consider when working with a developed site (and to avoid when building a new site) are:

1. Straight roads lead into the site rather than more pleasing, gently winding, natural roads that upon entrance would give a good first impression as your site literally "unfolds."
2. Cars and delivery vehicles intrude too far into the main site area; convenience has priority over aesthetics and safety.
3. Temporary facilities have become permanent.
4. Not enough outdoor meeting places are available for small and large groups.
5. Buildings are unimaginative, unattractive.
6. Porch decks, steps, and rustic benches are not provided to encourage enjoyment of the natural environment.
7. Sanitation systems are inadequate.
8. Electric lines detract from the natural beauty.
9. Trails are not provided in the natural outlying portions of the campsite. Campers experience only the main part of the site, which as a result is often overused.

Many times just a minor change such as rerouting a service road or changing the color of a building can greatly improve the appearance and function of a campsite.

THE LONG-RANGE (MASTER) SITE PLAN

Take time to plan. There can be so much excitement and hurry to have the camping program on the new site that adequate planning is forgotten or laid aside for later because of the time pressure. Existing camps likewise often seem content to plan as they go along.

1. Planning and maximum use of site. Long-range site planning should mean planning so that compatible programs can use different portions of the site at the same time without hindering the quality of any program. It should mean planning so that different programs can use the same facilities (or portion of the site) at different times (year-round use) without sacrificing quality. Except for very primitive wilderness camps, year-round use of sites is generally considered essential because high development and maintenance costs are hard to justify otherwise. Multi-use of the site and facilities permits maximum use and generates income.

2. *Planning and flexibility.* Long-range site planning should remain flexible. This is necessary because camp philosophy, to be relevant to the camper, often expresses itself in new ways. Because of this flexible characteristic, the term *development plan* might be better than *master plan.*

Any changes in the approved site development plan should be authorized by the camp board only after a careful study has been made of the total ramifications of the proposed change.

The long-range site plan should be reviewed in depth at least every five years.

3. *Planning and the camp program.* Long-range site planning should facilitate your program. Program enables you to reach your specific objectives in a way that expresses your philosophy of camping. The camp director (or program director) is the authority on a camp's program since he is usually its main architect. He is an important part of any long-range planning.

4. *Planning and the natural environment.* A long-range site planning should consider the natural environment. Soils, prevailing winds, sun patterns, and terrain are all basic considerations. The environment provides the backdrop for camp activities and is there to be observed and appreciated.

5. *Planning and implementation.* A long-range site plan should be written and should include implementation steps. The plan should clearly state the program and site considerations on which it is based. It should specify not only the exact location of a facility but also some of the rationale behind the facility's placement.

Implementation steps put a "handle" on the site plan. Based upon the camp's needs and priorities, they must represent a logical progression toward completion of the plan.

6. *Planning and continuity.* The long-range site plan ensures continuity and is a promotional, fund-raising tool. Only a written plan, understood and readily available to those who are responsible for the camp, can give the continuity that is necessary to complete a total plan. Leadership frequently changes, and a written site plan is

a stabilizing factor. The site plan along with maps, slides, and models is an aid in informing the camp's constituency and in raising financial support.

CAMP FACILITIES

FACILITIES REFLECT PHILOSOPHY.

Camper housing, for example, indicates the camp's philosophy of centralized or decentralized camping. Poorly constructed or maintained buildings imply the degree of importance leaders place on the camping ministry. Facilities, including activity areas, say much about the camp leadership's thinking about the camp experience.

FACILITIES SHOULD MEET STANDARDS.

Facility standards are provided by various organizations and levels of government to improve the quality of camping and to safeguard those participating. Since a quality experience and safety are also the camp's objectives, such standards, whether compulsory or voluntary, are of help to us.

Compulsory standards are the local, county, state, or federal laws that apply to the camp and its operation. These range from local zoning ordinances to federal Environmental Protection Agency (EPA) regulations. Legislation affecting youth camps varies greatly from state to state. It is important to become personally acquainted with local authorities, ask for specific requirements, give assurance that the camp wants to comply, and get their approval *before* beginning any construction.

As for voluntary standards, two large camping organizations provide important guidelines to encourage and measure excellence among camps: Christian Camping International (CCI) and the American Camping Association (ACA). The ACA requires that certain standards be met for camp membership. Through magazines and other educational efforts, including standards programs, both organizations have contributed greatly to raising the quality of camping.

Other organizations specialize in standards for activity areas, for instance, the American Red Cross (swimming and smallcraft), Camp Archery Association, and National Rifle Association.

FACILITIES RELATE TO ONE ANOTHER.

As an example of relating facilities, the caretaker residence relates directly to the maintenance shop. These both relate to the camp office. Again, the dining hall serves as a connecting link between the administrative cluster and camper living units. Activity areas relate primarily to the camper living units and the activity leaders' quarters.

Keeping in mind the guidance provided by program organization and natural environment, careful master planning will locate all facilities in a logical relationship to one another.

Site planners vary in their philosophy of planning. Some feel the "cluster" approach is best, that is, grouping related-function facilities near one another without crowding. This would tend to leave a large segment of the site in its natural state, thereby preserving wildlife habitats and plant communities. Campers could then enjoy these areas from trails provided for that purpose. Other planners prefer the "scattered" approach in which camp facilities are widespread over the entire site leaving few, if any, undisturbed natural areas.

While laying out the location of facilities and footpaths, an effective site plan will also visualize and spell out in considerable detail the location of various *functions* within buildings, especially the larger ones. This will enable the architect to design the building detail so that building relationships and pedestrian linkages are maintained.

FACILITIES SHOULD BE IMAGINATIVE, BEAUTIFUL, FUNCTIONAL.

It is of utmost importance that the camp buildings be compatible both with the natural surroundings and with each other. They should be imaginative and exciting, not merely functional, so that the developed site will be of such a quality as to exalt God, who created an exciting and imaginative natural world.

On the practical side, easy-to-maintain materials should be used, preferably those native to the site or that blend well with it.

As much use-flexibility as possible should be provided without losing a facility's suitability for its *primary* function. For example, the large, winterized lodge may serve primarily as the summer dining hall but also be planned to accommodate either one large retreat group or several smaller ones off-season with as little heat loss as possible.

Builders are not architects. A knowledge of camp structures is helpful, but more important is the ability to make a camp building exciting and unusual in its natural setting. If camp buildings are to be attractive, functional, and compatible with the site, the choice of an architect is crucial.

Maintaining Site and Facilities

Good stewardship of the camp investment would include a planned maintenance program. The caretaker must be given both the necessary tools and a place to work. An excellent resource for him would be Alan A. Nathans's *Handbook of Camp Maintenance* (see "Resources" at end of chapter).

Some camps have a building-by-building maintenance record system; others file by category (e.g., exterior painting). Whatever the system, it should be expressed in an orderly week-by-week (or monthly) work schedule. As development takes place, it is also the camp's responsibility to carefully document the location of all water, electric, and sanitation lines.

Often camp maintenance is thought of primarily in terms of buildings and activity areas, but we are stewards of the natural resources of our sites as well. Good conservation in the form of land, forest, water, and wildlife management is highly important. Overuse of any portion of the site should be recognized and corrected as quickly as possible. The United States Conservation Service is an excellent resource, and the agency's services are available for the asking.

SUGGESTIONS FOR STUDY

1. Visit a campsite and evaluate its primary activity area with regard to effective safeguards for the environment, locations of buildings for traffic and program efficiency, and overall impression of the development. Does it intrude on the setting or blend with it?
2. From the location and nature of structures, would you think the primary program emphasis in this camp is upon small or large group activity?
3. What is the function of a professional consultant in developing a new camp or upgrading an existing camp?
4. What factors should be considered when developing a long-range plan for a camp?
5. Identify the nine basic guidelines for evaluating a campsite.
6. Discuss the influence of campsite development on program.

RESOURCES

American Camping Association. *Camp Standards with Interpretations for Accreditation*. Martinsville, Ind.: ACA, 1975.

———. *Conservation of the Campsite*. Martinsville, Ind.: ACA, 1960.

———. *Use of Resident Camps for School Programs*. Martinsville, Ind.: ACA, 1972.

Athletic Institute, Inc. *Planning Facilities for Health, Physical Education and Recreation*. Chicago: Athletic Inst., 1956.

Boy Scouts of America. *Camp Sites and Facilities*. New York: BSA, 1965.

Camp Fire Girls, Inc. *Resident Camp Development*. New York: Camp Fire Girls, 1957.

Carpenter, Betty S. *Practical Family Campground Development and Operation*. Martinsville, Ind.: ACA, 1971.

Christian Camping International. *Foundations for Excellence*. Somonauk, Ill.: CCI, 1977.

Feechery, James M. *Camping for Senior Citizens*. Martinsville, Ind.: ACA, 1966.

Goodrich, Lois. *Decentralized Camping*. New York: Association, 1959.

Johnson, L. Ted, and Kingsley, Lee M. *Blueprint for Quality*. Chicago: Harvest, 1969.

Ledlie, John A., ed. *Developing Camp Sites and Facilities (YMCA)*. New York: Association, 1960.

Lykes, Ira B. *Recreational Vehicle Park Design and Management*. Mill Valley, Calif.: Rajo, 1970.

Nathans, Alan A. *Handbook of Camp Maintenance*. New York: Association, 1959.

Salomon, Julian H. *Campsite Development*. New York: Girl Scouts of Amer., 1966.

United Church Press. *Site Selection and Development*. Philadelphia: United Church, 1972.

15

Professional Camp Leadership

Bill V. Bynum

- *Chapter Assumptions*
- *Camping as a Profession*
- *Professional Training*

Professional—*quality and devoted performance in contrast to the amateur.*

BILL V. BYNUM (Ed.D., University of Southern California) is chairman of the Christian Education Department, Talbot Theological Seminary, La Mirada, California. Dr. Bynum's camping experience comprises eight years as a camp director; staff training for Green Oaks Ranch since 1963; CCI activity (two years as chairman of Educator's Committee and twice as representative to Orient for leadership development); and involvement in the camping program at Biola College.

The increasing growth of Christian camping throughout the world plus the developing of new operations and programs point up the necessity for professional leadership, and therefore professional education, in Christian camping. The preparation of the professional is among the newer aspects of this field, and the scope of this chapter is affected by this newness.

The chapter begins with several assumptions. These are followed by an overview of camping as a profession and a brief description of the concept of professional training.

Chapter Assumptions

This chapter is built upon several major premises. Some of these you may have already surmised as you have moved through the previous chapters.

1. Christian camping, professionally, is coming into its own and is establishing itself distinctively as a camping entity. It is better defined now than it has ever been and operationally and organizationally is making considerable strides.

2. As Christian camping moves through "professional birth pains," its definitions and expressions of professionalism will continue to change and mature. Such growth is aided by the involvement of Christian Camping International and the desire of the leaders in the Christian camping field to effect a genuinely biblical concept of leadership. The student of Christian camping desiring to prepare himself for participation in the field can contribute to this growth through research, insight, and innovative action.

3. If Christian camping is to be an arm of the church, it needs to work at its potential now, rather than waiting for the next generation to accomplish the challenges of today. It is encouraging that those in leadership desire to see the field develop professionally and that men and women be professionally prepared to minister effectively through camping.

4. Professionalism does not necessitate a disregard for the spiritual distinctives of Christian camping. The commitment to Christ and the Word of God, the ministry of bringing persons into a relationship with Christ and a new life-style—these are still elements that must permeate the personal and professional life of the individual entering this field.

5. The world is the field. Professional leadership development must include those principles and concepts that prepare individuals for competent service in other cultures. This should discourage the establishment of training that is centered in programs rather

than in principles, in promotion and property rather than in people.
6. Finally, the approach in this chapter is explorative in nature. There is still lack of definition in many areas, and it will be important not to finalize some aspects of professional training too soon. It is to be hoped that those teaching in the field will also be challenged to explore, ponder, interact, and project in such a manner as to contribute meaningfully to this development of Christian camping professionally. In this connection, note the suggestions for study given at the conclusion of the chapter.

CAMPING AS A PROFESSION

Validation of *camping* as a professional field needs little or no defense. Consideration of *Christian camping* as a professional field, however, though generally accepted, deserves specific inquiry and clarification. Professions tend to define themselves with a basic formula or series of questions. These questions include:
1. Is there a general recognition of the field as a profession?
2. Is there a specific body of knowledge about which the field revolves?
3. Is basic research being done in the particular field?
4. What are the specific training programs, and are they professionally oriented and in higher education?
5. Does the field offer any accepted certification?
6. Are personnel standards available and recognized?
7. What is being done specifically in recruitment to the profession?
8. Does the field have any professional organization(s)?
9. Is there a recognized code of ethics?

From the reading of previous chapters, it would seem clear that Christian camping professionally is lacking or weak in several of the areas listed. Certification is one example. This weakness should, however, be challenging rather than discouraging because of the opportunities for growth that it presents.

RECOGNITION AS A PROFESSION

Since the establishment of Christian Camping International, and because of its efforts to synthesize individual camp and denominational efforts, the perspective of professional leadership has changed. This change can be seen in the new attitude of church, community, and both local and federal government. The influence of the Christian camp director and board members noticeably improved in the seventies. Many denominations now have camp or camp-oriented committees or commissions. The corporate strength of Christian camping leadership through CCI is growing.

The directory of Christian Camping International indicates a constantly growing listing of men and women as full-time employees in the field of Christian camping. In addition, a considerable number of volunteers assist in Christian camps.

PROFESSIONAL EDUCATION

The status of professional education is rapidly changing. In the 1970s special growth was achieved in this area. During the previous decade, many Bible institutes and colleges, as well as several Christian liberal arts colleges, had a course or two in camping. These were generally "catchall" courses. At the same time a few camps, cooperating with colleges, offered training programs with credit attached for their precamp training and summer ministry.

The beginning of the 1970s showed development of programs that were more professionally oriented. The physical education departments of liberal arts schools, for example, began to divide courses involving both recreation and camping into separate courses of study. A number of schools developed programs legitimately professional in nature. Although some sought to use camping in the preparation of leaders for several fields, others designed programs for the full-time camp administrator. Examples of such programs can be seen in the Honey Rock Camp program of Wheaton College, Wheaton, Illinois, and in the camping major at Biola College, LaMirada, California. More recently developed are the programs at Le Tourneau College, Longview, Texas, and Calvary Bible College, Kansas City, Missouri.

The relative newness of these training programs, plus the fact that few camps make a professional degree mandatory for the top staff positions, suggest the pioneer nature of training for professional leadership in Christian camping. However, with the growing complexity of our culture, leaders in the Christian camping field are being made increasingly aware of the necessity for such professional training.

The design of leader training, reflecting each school's concept of camping, will vary from school to school. Efforts are being made to standardize basic courses so that their quality and content have a professional level. The Education Committee of Christian Camping International has been involved in such efforts.

Although the camping field is attractive to Christian youth concerned with contemporary ministry, the demands of the field vocationally do not appear at this time to warrant extensive educational programming on a widespread basis. It is also apparent that the limited number of students seriously considering such programs is a major question for school administrators.

RESEARCH IN CHRISTIAN CAMPING

Christian camping continues to fall short in the area of research within higher education. Although there is some growth in the area of curriculum development, at the present time broad research is rather limited.

Graduate programs such as the MA in Christian Education (or MRE in some cases) as well as advanced studies in Christian ministries offer hope that course and thesis research opportunities related to camping will increase.

Consideration has been given to setting up through CCI a central data bank on available camping research. Also, abstracts of presentations given at international and regional camping conventions are envisioned as a part of this projected service.

Development of curricula for professional training in camping is becoming more definitive and more specifically related to the major responsibilities of the various levels of camp leadership. Courses related to camp management, personnel, program, facility, communication, and teaching-counseling functions are becoming more common. In many courses theory is blended with practice, thereby allowing camping skills to be mastered on a more experientially based approach.

CERTIFICATION OF PERSONNEL

Personnel certification in Christian camping is an area also suffering "birth pains." CCI is the logical group through which personnel certification would be established for evangelical camps. There is no specific certification at this point, although some expression of standards is given in CCI's *Foundations for Excellence.*

STANDARDS WITHIN CHRISTIAN CAMPING

With reference to personnel, few positions are genuinely standardized throughout Christian camps. The standardizing of salaries, for example, is as difficult in camps as within churches. Consequently, a broad field of endeavor lies before the student of camping as position titles, job descriptions, tenure, and salary comparisons are explored.

Some positions emerging professionally at this point would include the executive director, assistant or program director, and program specialists. Positions related to services outside the program area tend to be viewed as paraprofessional.

Hiring practices and staff policies are being more closely spelled out by the larger camps and conferences, and many now have manuals with well-defined personnel policies.

RECRUITMENT OF STAFF

Staff recruitment is also an aspect of the professional status. Employment opportunities can be discovered through CCI, particularly by means of its *Journal of Christian Camping*. A referral service for Christian camps has been incorporated into the computer placement program of Intercristo (Box 9323, Seattle, WA 98101). Interest in camping grows among mission agencies at home and abroad, and major referral has been through Intercristo. The past decade has witnessed an increasing number of mission agencies that list "camping specialist" among their job titles.

Another growing area of interest is the larger church that operates its own camp. To an increasing degree, churches are becoming concerned that men and women being considered for youth ministries have a background in camping.

PROFESSIONAL ORGANIZATIONS

The major professional organization for evangelical camps is Christian Camping International, headquartered at Somonauk, Illinois. Membership embraces several broad categories: camp or conference, school, church library, personal (including student), and business or consultant.

The major CCI purposes include mutual strengthening through sharing among members, upgrading the camping ministry through the *Foundations for Excellence* certification and growth program, and providing resource material for leadership through monographs, research, and the bimonthly *Journal of Christian Camping*. CCI provides a variety of consultant services through its staff and associated resource persons. Area, regional, national, and international conventions serve the membership, which includes five national divisions and more than forty countries.

In addition, many directors and other staff members in Christian camps are active in the American Camping Association. Several major denominations also have camping associations which encourage individual, camp, and church participation. Professional growth in camping is being advanced through these associations.

LEVELS OF SERVICE

The various levels of professional service, though not yet clearly delineated, might be classified as executive level, supervisory level, and program level.

The executive level would refer primarily to positions of administrative leadership for which the highest level of training and experience is desirable. The executive director, program director, and business manager would likely fall into this category.

The supervisory level would describe those with specialized responsibilities in the supervision of staff persons at a larger camp.

The program level would involve those who work closely with the campers as program specialists. Included would be the waterfront specialist, the recreation specialist, and the craft director. While the unit counselor is perhaps the most influential staff member as far as the camper is concerned, the nature of the position renders it paraprofessional.

Caution should be taken when differentiating levels since circumstances in camps vary greatly. A professional post in one camp might be classified as paraprofessional in another. For the purpose of this chapter, *paraprofessioanal* is used to describe those positions and responsibilities that are specialized and are more at the operational level as compared to the administrative level. These might include counseling, health, food, business, and informational and maintenance services. These may, of course, be full-time in larger camps. The use of the term *paraprofessional* does not imply that these positions require less than professional competence but rather that they involve technical skills and training.

PROFESSIONAL TRAINING

A profession requires educational opportunity at both undergraduate and graduate levels. In Christian camping there are two major *philosophies of training and preparation* under which educational programs are being developed.

One concept is that which Wheaton College's Camp Honey Rock follows. Here, camping is included in general preparation for leadership in whatever field an individual chooses to enter. Consequently the program puts strong emphasis on the personal camping experience and uses this for the camping development of the individual.

The other philosophy is more directly related to camping. Primarily it is concerned with the development of specific skills and their immediate application to the operation of a Christian camp. Such is the pattern followed by Biola, Le Tourneau, and Calvary Bible Colleges.

Paraprofessional training is generally best accomplished through the summer training opportunities offered by many camps. The individual has opportunity to concentrate in a specific area and develop skills and concepts essential to that area of camping.

Some camps use a rotating system with their summer staff, thereby providing experience in several areas during the season. This approach provides the camp with needed personnel on a short-term basis and gives the novice valuable opportunities to explore the camping profession in an on-the-job manner.

As a consequence of these summer ministries, there is a growing relationship between camps and colleges. This relationship is greatly enhanced by the development of specialized training programs, particularly in well-defined internship programs.

In some situations the student can receive college credit for summer in-service training. Training patterns vary, as do the number of unit or hour academic credits allowed.

These educational programs revolve around the study of the Scriptures and the application of biblical principles to the functioning of a camp. In addition to this concern for biblical foundations is the study of program structure so that camping principles and skills are developed. The challenge is to balance the practical and theoretical and to develop the training at academic levels consistent with professionalism, while providing an optimum of on-site experience.

Such balance between the theoretical and the practical suggests that as much of the training be provided on location as in the classroom. This arrangement not only strengthens the relationships between camps and colleges but also makes possible expanding the camp ministry to incorporate an "apprenticeship" approach to training.

An example of such a pattern is seen in the program of Biola College (See box.)

Biola College Camping Major

PURPOSE: To prepare the graduate for supervisory leadership in the camping profession by assisting him:

1. To discover and develop personal gifts and respective strengths and abilities, especially those related to the camping profession;
2. To demonstrate his awareness of the camping environment and his sensitivity to persons as reflected in his philosophy and practice;
3. To demonstrate his understanding of, appreciation of, and ability in using the personal growth of self and others;
4. To demonstrate his understanding of and ability in using administrative principles by effectively managing camping operations and effectively and educationally leading others.

Pre-requisites: Introduction to Camping (2)
                Human Development (3)

Major requirements:

Administration:	Educational Administration	(5)
	Camp Administration	(2)
	Recreation Administration	(2)
	Recreation Leadership	(2)
Education:	Education Psychology	(3)
	Camp Education Skills	(8)
Interpersonal Relationships:	Camp Counseling	(2)
	Group Communications	(3)
Safety:	(First aid, and CPR, along with other safety skills, are taught in Intro. to Camping. Bio. 152—Applied Anatomy may be taken as part of the General Ed. science requirement.)	
Intregration:	Educational, Psychological and Social Foundations	(3)
	Supervised Field Study	(3)
Electives:	Complete the degree requirements with all units totaling 130.	

From this statement of objectives and a review of the program design, it will be noted that this approach to undergraduate training concentrates on preparing the student for camp supervisory positions.

In the area of training paraprofessionals, the possibility of developing programs to prepare individuals for food service, maintenance, and business administration is being considered by camping leaders. Consideration here is that such a program might parallel professional training programs.

Graduate programming in general is presently moving to incorporate training in specialized areas, such as programming for special needs: the physically and mentally handicapped, senior adults, and similar areas. It also considers site planning and development, business administration, public relations and publicity, and more intense study of the philosophical and psychological impacts of the camping experience.

A major concern for any program seeking to develop leadership for Christian camping would be the *field of internship concept*. This begins with the experience offered by many camps through counselor-in-training (CIT) programs. Whether the program revolves around maintenance, counseling, recreation, or a combination of these, field experience is a major training opportunity.

A growing number of camps offer specialized training programs under the title *internship*. This training approach takes the student with previous experience and developing expertise and allows him to work somewhat as an apprentice to a senior staff member.[1]

The breadth and depth of camping internship experience varies, but the approach is basically the same: strong interpersonal relationships that exemplify the discipling concept in both the spiritual and vocational aspects of the student's life.

Professional camp leadership training in a Christian context is available in a limited but increasing amount. Like other areas of professional education there are struggles with theory and practice, classroom education and field training, the "how to" and the "why," and the educator and the practitioner. But there is encouraging progress that augers well for the quality status of Christian camping in the future.

---

1. See chapter 8, "Training Programs: A Case Study."

SUGGESTIONS FOR STUDY

1. What major areas of development and concern in Christian camping have had the most effect upon leadership training? (Refer to previous chapters for background.)
2. What dangers are potentially a part of the growth of any profession? What would help prevent problems in this area for the Christian leader?
3. How would you define paraprofessional in relation to Christian camping? What major differences are there in preparation of the professional and the paraprofessional?
4. What functions do you see for Christian Camping International in the developing of the field professionally? In what ways might CCI be assisted in this through the colleges?
5. Describe camp training opportunities within commuting distance from your school.
6. From your perspective at this point, list and rank those areas of camping training you feel most vital in your own personal and professional growth.
7. Design a self-improvement program for camp leadership that could be put into operation now. This should incorporate educational opportunities within your academic program but must also include the use of other means for growth. Consider carefully your goals and resources.
8. Develop a chart comparing camping courses offered by various schools. This could be extended to include field training and courses offered for credit through camps.
9. Interview several camp directors and other staff to ascertain their education and personal leadership needs. Summarize the data and indicate inferences derived from the interviews that could assist in the design of curriculum for professional training.
10. Contact mission boards and agencies to discover how training might be developed to be more applicable in a cross-cultural context.
11. Set up a comparative study of staff (professional) titles, job descriptions, salaries, and length of tenure, through contact with a random sampling of camps using a questionnaire and studying staff manuals. Include in the study an investigation into the education and experience required for the positions.

Appendix

Camping Organizations

For many years the American Camping Association and the Canadian Camping Association have served the broad camping movement of these nations, including many Christian camps. However, the distinctive needs and interests of evangelical Christian camps and conferences began to draw leaders together in several parts of the U.S. and Canada as early as the 40's and 50's. These gatherings were casual and sporadic at best, but in the 60's several influences stirred representatives of the informal regional camping fellowships to explore the possibilities for a national association. The discoveries of this exploration led finally to Christian Camping International, a thriving, growing fellowship of camp-minded people from more than 50 nations around the world.

CCI publishes the *Journal of Christian Camping*, an essential tool for the leader or student of camping. Sectional, national, and international conventions pool the experience and enthusiam of camping's best leaders. Participation in CCI would seem indispensible to all who are serious about the ministry of camps and conferences.

Christian Camping International—Canada
745 Mt. Pleasant Road
Toronto, Ontario M4S 2N5

Christian Camping International—U.S.
P.O. Box 646
Wheaton, IL 60187
For information on CCI organizations overseas, contact the CCI-U.S. office.

American Camping Association
Bradford Woods
Martinsville, IN 46151

Canadian Camping Association
Suite 2
1806 Avenue Road
Toronto, Ontario M5M 3Z1

Camping Resources

Each chapter includes a bibliography. However, several titles that are listed have gone out of print, but may be located in libraries. For a listing of available titles and new books that have appeared since 1979, request the book catalogs issued by Christian Camping International, the American Camping Association, and the Canadian Camping Association.

Camping Guideposts

Camping Guideposts was founded in 1981 to serve program and leadership needs for Christian camps. More than 500 camps, conferences, schools, and Christian agencies representing practically every denomination and region of the U.S. and Canada use Camping Guideposts training and program materials. A free newsletter lists resources and reports on developments in the Christian camping literature field. The books listed below, as well as the newsletter, may be secured by writing or calling Camping Guideposts, 5118 Glendale Street, Duluth, MN 55804. (218) 525-3235.

Mattson, Lloyd. *The Camp Counselor.* Duluth: Camping Guideposts, 1983 (Rev.). A 192-page training manual for counselors, with self-study guide.

Graendorf, Werner C., and Mattson, Lloyd D., Eds. *Introduction to Christian Camping.* Duluth: Camping Guideposts, 1984 (Rev.).

Barnett, Timothy L., Flora, Steven B. *Christian Outdoor Education.* Duluth: Camping Guideposts, 1982. The philosophy and methodology for conducting outdoor education for Christian schools and camps.

Barnett, Timothy L., and Flora, Steven B. *Exploring God's Web of Life.* Duluth: Camping Guideposts, 1982. A teacher's manual for Christian outdoor education.

Mattson, Lloyd and Elsie. *Rediscover Your Family Outdoors*, Wheaton: Victor Books, 1980. Family values in camping and outdoor activity.

Mattson, Lloyd. *Cabin/Trail Devotions.* Duluth: Camping Guideposts, 1981—A series of camp Bible study plans integrating small-group study with the camper's quiet time, cabin devotions, and home follow-up. Each title contains six studies.

Mattson, Lloyd. *Build Your Church Through Camping.* Duluth: Camping Guideposts, 1984. A 48-page discussion of values for the church and the church worker to be found in the Bible camp.

Mattson, Lloyd. *The Apples In a Seed.* Duluth: Camping Guideposts, 1983. A camp case history, the story of Camp Haluwasa, New Jersey.